TALK

German

SUSANNE WINCHESTER

Series Editor: Alwena Lamping

BBC Active, an imprint of Educational Publishers LLP, part of the Pearson Education Group, Edinburgh Gate, Harlow, Essex CM20 2JE, England

First published 2012.
5 4 3 2

ISBN 978-1-4066-7913-7

Cover design: adapted from original artwork by
Helen Williams and Matt Bookman
Cover photograph: © Richard Boll/GETTYIMAGES
Insides design: Nicolle Thomas, Rob Lian
Layout: Pantek Media Ltd. www.pantekmedia.co.uk
Illustrations © Mark Duffin
Publisher: Debbie Marshall
Development editor: Sue Purcell
Project editor: Emma Brown
Marketing: Paul East
Senior production controller: Franco Forgione

Audio producer: Colette Thomson, Footstep Productions Ltd.
Sound engineer: Andrew Garratt
Presenters: Walter Bohnacker, Britta Gartner, Angelika Libera, Fernando Tiberini

Printed and bound in China (CTPSC/02).

The Publisher's policy is to use paper manufactured from sustainable forests.

Contents

Introduction

Talk German 2 is a new course from BBC Active, helping you to improve your German in an enjoyable and stimulating way. It's designed for people who have some experience of German – whether from an introductory course (such as the bestselling **Talk German**), a first-level class or time spent in Germany – and who want to build on what they've learnt.

Recognising that language is reinforced through repetition, **Talk German 2** takes time to revisit the basics, as well as taking you forward at a sensible and manageable pace. The course deals with interesting, adult topics such as food and wine, getting to know people, finding out about German property, shopping and coping with problems. It's ideal, whether you want to learn for work or for fun, and as preparation for a national Level 1 qualification. The course covers the preliminary level of the Languages Ladder.

What makes **Talk German 2** special?
- It has been developed by a team of professionals with extensive experience in adult language learning.
- The carefully designed activities focus on all the dimensions of learning German and aim to develop your ability to speak the language, understand replies, and experiment with reading and writing in German.
- It recognises that, in order to go beyond basic phrases and really express yourself, you'll need to know some German grammar. And it presents the grammar in a way that's easy to understand, without jargon or complex technical explanations.
- It incorporates highly effective learning strategies, such as predicting, educated guesswork, memory building, gist reading and selective use of a glossary.
- Its structured and systematic approach promotes steady progress and a real sense of achievement, boosting your confidence as well as your linguistic ability.

Talk German 2, which includes this book and 140 minutes of audio recordings by native German speakers, is an interactive course, involving you at all the stages of the learning process.

Wherever you see this: **1•5**, the phrases or dialogues are recorded on the CD (i.e. CD1, track 5).

Talk German 2 consists of:

Units 1 to 10, each containing:

- *In Deutschland*, an insight into German culture to set your learning in context;
- summaries of key language for you to listen to, read and repeat to practise your pronunciation;
- activities designed around the audio recordings, to develop your listening skills and understanding;
- succinct *Auf Deutsch* explanations of how the language works, placed exactly where you need the information (where appropriate, these are expanded in the grammar section at the back – see links e.g. **G15**);
- a *Put it all together* section, consolidating what you've learnt before you put it to the test in *Now you're talking*, where you are prompted to speak German;
- a final progress check with a quiz and a checklist summarising key points.

Noch Mehr! supplements, at regular intervals, which will:

- take you that little bit further, reinforcing and extending what you've learnt in the two preceding units;
- broaden your vocabulary and/or place words that you know into a new context;
- develop your reading and writing skills.

A comprehensive reference section:

- a set of clear definitions of essential grammar terms (on page 6)
- transcripts of all the audio material
- answers to the activities
- a guide to pronunciation and spelling
- a grammar section
- German-English glossary
- English-German glossary.

BBC Active would like to thank all the language tutors who contributed to the planning of the **Talk 2** series. Our particular thanks go to Pam Lander Brinkley MA (Ed) and Sue Maitland, York ACES (Adult and Community Education Service).

Glossary of grammatical terms

To make the most of the *Auf Deutsch* notes, it helps to know the meaning of the following key grammatical terms:

- **Nouns** are the words for people, places, concepts and things: *son, doctor, sheep, house, Scotland, time, freedom.*
- **Gender** Every German noun is either masculine, feminine or neuter, as are any articles and adjectives that relate to it.
- **Articles** are *the* (definite article) and *a/an* (indefinite article).
- **Pronouns** avoid the need to repeat nouns: *it, them, you, they.*
- **Singular** means one.
- **Plural** means more than one.
- **Case** refers to the role that a noun or pronoun plays in a sentence. In German there are four cases, each one associated with a different role: nominative, accusative, dative and genitive.
- **Adjectives** describe nouns: *German* wine, the children are *small*.
- **Adverbs** add information to adjectives and verbs: *very* big, to speak *slowly*.
- **Verbs** are words like *to go, to sleep, to eat, to like, to have, to be*, that refer to doing and being.
- **Infinitive** German verbs are listed in a dictionary in the infinitive form, ending in -**en**. The English equivalent is *to*: *to eat, to have*.
- **Regular verbs** follow a predictable pattern, while **irregular verbs** don't.
- The **person** of a verb indicates who or what is doing something:
  1st person = the speaker: *I* (singular), *we* (plural)
  2nd person = the person(s) being addressed: *you*
  3rd person = who/what is being talked about: *he/she/it/they*
- The **tense** of a verb indicates when something is done, e.g. in the past (*I worked, I was working*) now (*I work*) or in the future (*I will work*).
- The **subject** of a sentence is the person/thing carrying out the verb: *they* have two children, *Anna* reads the paper.
- The **object** of a sentence is at the receiving end of a verb: they have *two children*, Anna reads *the paper*.
- A **clause** is a group of words containing a subject and a verb and forming part of a sentence.

Ich liebe Deutschland!

getting to know people

giving information about people

talking about work

explaining why you're learning German

In Deutschland ...

a popular way of learning German is to go on a **Sprachreise** *language study trip* in Germany, for example staying with a **Gastfamilie** *host family* and attending a **Sprachkurs** *language course* in a **Sprachschule** *language school* during the day. It's an excellent way to practise the language whilst learning more about the **Kultur** – **Musik**, **Geschichte** *history*, **Architektur** – and **Traditionen**.

Sport and **Freizeit** *leisure* play an important role in German life, so there's no shortage of **Freizeitangebote** *leisure activities* to keep your body and mind active.

Getting to know people

1 1•03 Listen to the key language:

Wie heißt du?	What's your name?
Ich heiße ...	I'm called ...
Bist du ...?	Are you (informal) ...?
Ich bin ...	I'm ...
Woher kommst du?	Where do you come from?
Ich komme aus ...	I come from ...
in der Nähe von ...	near/in the vicinity of ...
Wo wohnst du?	Where do you live?
Ich wohne in/mit ...	I live in/with ...

2 1•04 At the start of a **Sprachkurs** in Freiburg, the teacher suggests: **Sollen wir uns duzen?** *Shall we say du to each other?* Until you hear this, it's better to use the more formal **Sie**. The teacher, rather than introduce herself, invites people to ask her some questions. Listen and make a note of her first name and where she lives.

Name .... *Zimmermann*   **Wohnort** ....

3 1•05 Tom and Eva, two of the people on the course, are getting to know each other. Listen and fill the gaps in their conversation. Eva starts by saying *Pleased to meet you*.

- Hallo, ich ...... Tom.
- Freut mich, Tom. ...... du Engländer?
- Nein, ich ...... Amerikaner. Und du? Wie ...... du?
- Eva.
- Woher ...... du?
- Ich .... aus Warschau in Polen. Ich bin Polin, aber ich ...... in Deutschland.
- Und ich wohne ...... meinem Bruder ...... England, in der Nähe ...... Bristol.

Auf Deutsch

In a more formal setting, **Sie** would be used instead of **du**: du wohnst, du heißt, du kommst would become **Sie wohnen, Sie heißen, Sie kommen.**

4 Have a go at introducing yourself, giving your name and nationality and saying where you live.

Giving information about people

1 **1•06** Listen to the key language:

Darf ich ... vorstellen?	May I introduce ...?
er/sie heißt ...	he/she is called ...
er/sie wohnt ...	he/she lives ...
sie wohnen ...	they live ...
er/sie ist ...	he/she is ...
sie sind ...	they are ...
Hast du ...?	Do you have ...?
sie haben ...	they have ...

2 **1•07** Eva and Tom have been asked to introduce each other to the rest of the group. Tom lives **mit seinem Bruder** *with his brother*. Have another look at their conversation on page 8 and see if you could introduce them, then listen to how they do it and compare the two.

The ending of a verb changes from the infinitive ending **-(e)n** depending on who/what is involved. For many verbs, such as **wohnen** *to live*, the endings are regular and predictable:

ich wohne	*I live*
du wohnst	*you (informal, sing) live*
er/sie/es wohnt	*he/she/it lives*
wir wohnen	*we live*
ihr wohnt	*you (informal, plural of du) live*
sie/Sie wohnen	*they/you (formal, sing/pl) live* **G20**

Auf Deutsch

3 **1•08** Eva's group carry on with their questions. Listen then decide whether the following facts about her are true or false. **Ihr** means *her*; it has masculine and feminine endings – **ihr Mann** *her husband* and **ihre Tochter** *her daughter*.

	richtig	falsch
a Stefanie ist verheiratet.		
b Ihr Mann heißt Olaf.		
c Sie haben vier Kinder.		
d Ihre Tochter heißt Susanne.		
e Ihre Tochter ist vierzehn Jahre alt.		

Now write the correct version of any that are false. You might need the transcript on page 107.

Talking about work

1 **1●09** Listen to the key language:

Was bist du von Beruf?	What do you do?
Ich arbeite als ...	I work as ...
Ich arbeite bei/für ...	I work at/for ...
... von zuhause	... from home
Ich bin ... (von Beruf).	I am a/an ... (by profession).
seit 2002/seit dreizehn Jahren	since 2002/for 13 years

2 **1●10** Use the glossary to find the German word for the illustrations, making sure that you use the correct masculine or feminine version. Then listen to people talking about what they do and tick the occupations you hear mentioned.

Kellner(in)
Arzt/Ärztin
Klempner(in)
Friseur(in)
Journalist(in)
Tischler(in)
Redakteur(in)
Buchhalter(in)

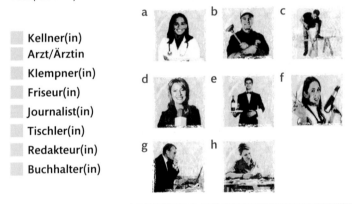

To say you've been doing something for a period of time or since a particular time, you use **seit** and the present tense.
Ich wohne seit Februar in Bremen. *I've been living in Bremen since February.*
Ich arbeite seit 2005 in Deutschland. *I've been working in Germany since 2005.*
A reference to time usually comes before a reference to place.

3 **1●11** Listen and underline the correct information.

a Claudia has been working as a press officer for an airline since 2000 / 2002 / 2003.

b Rainer has been an estate agent for 3 / 13 / 30 years.

Explaining why you're learning German

1 **1•12** Listen to the key language:

Warum lernst du Deutsch?	Why are you learning German?
Ich mag (noun).	I like ...
Ich mag Sprachen.	I like languages.
Ich (verb) **gern.**	I like ...(-ing).
Ich höre gern Opernmusik.	I like listening to opera.
Ich reise (sehr) gern.	I like travelling (very much).
Ich liebe ...	I love ...
Weil ich Deutschland liebe!	Because I love Germany!

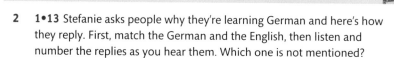

2 **1•13** Stefanie asks people why they're learning German and here's how they reply. First, match the German and the English, then listen and number the replies as you hear them. Which one is not mentioned?

a	Ich mag die deutsche Kultur.	1	I like German beer.
b	Weil ich Sprachen mag.	2	Because I like languages.
c	Weil ich Deutschland liebe!	3	Out of curiosity – that's all!
d	Ich möchte in Österreich arbeiten.	4	I like travelling very much.
e	Ich reise sehr gern.	5	I'd like to work in Austria.
f	Ich möchte deutsche Bücher lesen.	6	I like German culture.
g	Aus Neugier – das ist alles!	7	I like listening to opera.
h	Ich höre gern Opernmusik.	8	Because I love Germany!
i	Ich mag das deutsche Bier.	9	I'd like to read German books.

> When there are two verbs in a clause, the second (the infinitive) goes at the end: Ich <u>möchte</u> in Deutschland <u>arbeiten</u>.
> The verb also goes at the end after **weil** *because*:
> Ich lerne Deutsch, weil ich Deutschland liebe.
>
> **G21**

Auf
Deutsch

3 **1•14** Joan's learning because her son is married to a German girl. Listen and see if you can pick out what her daughter-in-law's name is and where she's from.
Name ....   **Stadt** ....

4 Using a dictionary if necessary, work out how to say why you're learning German.

put it all together

1 Match the German and the English.

a	Ich mag das deutsche Bier.	1	I like working in Germany.
b	Wie heißt sie?	2	I like German beer.
c	Ich möchte in Deutschland arbeiten.	3	For five years.
d	Ich mag die deutsche Musik.	4	What's your name?
e	Ich arbeite gern in Deutschland.	5	I'd like to work in Germany.
f	Wie heißen Sie?	6	What is she called?
g	Seit fünf Jahren.	7	I like German music.

2 Write down the missing forms of the regular verbs **trinken** *to drink*, **machen** *to do/make* and **zahlen** *to pay* in the table below. Even though you might not yet have come across them, you should still be able to predict the endings.

	ich	du	er/sie/es	wir	ihr	sie/Sie
trinken		trinkst			trinkt	
machen	mache			machen		
zahlen			zahlt			zahlen

3 Here's a profile of a graphic designer from Bremen.

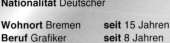

Nachname Meister **Vorname** Robert
Geburtsdatum
3. Dezember 1975
Nationalität Deutscher

Wohnort Bremen   **seit** 15 Jahren
Beruf Grafiker   **seit** 8 Jahren

   a How might he introduce himself? Use all the information and give his age in 2012.
   b And how would you introduce him to a group of people? *He's a designer* is **Er ist Grafiker von Beruf**.

4 Now think of two people you know and practise introducing them to others.

now you're talking!

1 **1•15** You're going to be asked these questions. Answer them as if you were Christine Carpenter, who's been working as a photographer for the past seven years. She's learning German because she likes travelling.

> **Nachname** Carpenter
> **Vorname** Christine
> **Nationalität** Engländerin
> **Wohnort** Brighton
> **Beruf** Fotografin

- Hallo! Wie heißt du?
- Bist du Amerikanerin?
- Woher in England kommst du?
- Was bist du von Beruf?
- Seit wann bist du Fotografin?
- Warum möchtest du Deutsch lernen?

2 **1•16** Now it's your turn to ask the questions. You're in a queue with someone about your age and you start a conversation by saying *Hi* and asking what he is called.

- Jürgen – Jürgen Donner. Freut mich.
- ◆ Ask Jürgen where he comes from.
- Ich komme aus Köln *Cologne*.
- ◆ Find out whether he's living in Cologne.
- Nein. Ich wohne seit 2008 in Lübeck.
- ◆ Ask what he does for a living.
- Ich bin Grafiker. Ich arbeite von zuhause, weil ich eine kleine Tochter habe.
- ◆ Ask how old she is.
- Sie ist vierzehn Monate alt und sehr süß.

quiz

1 If someone says **Sollen wir uns duzen**, what are they suggesting?

2 How would you introduce Klaus to a group of people?

3 When you're talking about yourself, what letter does the verb generally end in?

4 Which form of **sein** is needed here: **Mein Bruder ......
Amerikaner** – do you need **bin**, **ist** or **sind** in the gap?

5 What's the German for a female plumber?

6 If you've been working in York since 1998, what word will you need to insert here? **Ich arbeite ...... 1998 in York.**

7 Would you use **Ich möchte reisen** or **Ich reise gern** to say you like travelling?

8 What are **Sprachen**?

Now check whether you can ...

- introduce yourself
- say where you live and what you do for a living
- say how long you've been doing these
- explain why you're learning German
- ask people their names, what they do and where they live
- introduce someone
- provide information about where he/she lives and works

Successful language learning requires a great deal of practice, consolidation and revision – but all this is made easier by making what you're learning relevant to you personally. So, why not get your dictionary and start to boost your vocabulary by creating as many sentences as you can starting with **Ich bin**, **Ich mag**, **Ich möchte**, **Ich liebe**.

Um halb neun

saying what happens using the 24-hour clock

... and the informal 12-hour clock

talking about daily routine

... and the working day

In Deutschland ...

although the 24-hour clock is widely used in formal situations such as timetables or business appointments, you'll also come across the 12-hour clock in informal everyday speech. You can tell the time either by stating the hour followed by **Uhr** and the minutes: **drei Uhr zwanzig** *3.20*, or you can use **nach** for minutes past the hour and **vor** for minutes to the hour: **Viertel nach neun** *quarter past nine*; **zwanzig vor zehn** *twenty to ten*. **Halb** is *half*, but beware: while in English the half-hour is counted on top of the full hour, in German you express how much time there is left until the next hour, so *half past seven* is **halb acht** (i.e. halfway to eight o'clock).

You can use **morgens/mittags/nachmittags/abends/nachts** *in the morning/at lunchtime/in the afternoon/in the evening/at night* if clarification is needed: **um halb sechs morgens** *at 5.30 in the morning*.

Using the 24-hour clock

1 **1•18** Listen to the key language:

Es gibt einen Flug um …	There's a flight at …
Der nächste Flug geht um …	The next one goes at …
Mein Flug kommt um … an.	My flight arrives at …
von … bis …	from … until
Es tut mir leid.	I'm sorry.

2 **1•19** Ricardo Silva has missed his flight to Berlin. Complete the information he's given at check-in, and make a note of what time the next three flights leave, even though the first is **voll** *full*.

◆ **Es gibt einen Flug um …. nach Berlin, aber er ist voll; es gibt leider** *unfortunately* **keine Plätze mehr.**

● **Und der nächste Flug?**

◆ **Der nächste Flug geht um …. und ein anderer geht um ….**

● **Gibt es einen Flug vor** *before* **….?**

◆ **Nein, leider nicht.**

Auf Deutsch

Separable verbs are verbs with a prefix added, which alters the meaning: **kommen** *to come*; **ankommen** *to arrive*. If a separable verb is the only verb in a sentence, the prefix is separate and goes at the end of the sentence. When there are two verbs, the separable verb stays intact and goes in the infinitive at the end.
Wir <u>kommen</u> um sieben Uhr <u>an</u>.
Ich möchte am Montag <u>ankommen</u>.
Er <u>ruft</u> um halb drei <u>an</u>. (**anrufen** *to call/telephone*)   G18–20

3 **1•20** Ricardo's in Germany for a **Konferenz** *conference*. Listen as he rings Martin Droste, a colleague, and leaves him a message. What time does he say his flight will be arriving? …………

4 At the last minute, the airline got Ricardo on the earlier flight. How would he let Martin know that he'll be arriving at 6.25pm?
Es tut mir leid, aber es gibt eine Planänderung. Ich ……..

5 Ricardo receives this message from Martin, asking him to call him from Berlin airport. What are the missing words?
Herr Silva, ich habe von 16.00 bis 18.30 Termine *appointments*. **Bitte … Sie mich vom Flughafen Berlin … Bis später** (lit. *until later;* **spät** *late*).

... and the informal 12-hour clock

6 **1•21** Listen to the key language:

um Viertel nach zehn	at a quarter past ten
um Viertel vor elf	at a quarter to eleven
um halb elf	at half past ten
bis sieben Uhr abends	until seven in the evening
nach Hause	home; to my/your etc. house

In the main part of a sentence (i.e. the main clause), the verb is always the second element – which does not necessarily mean the second word. If the subject (s) of the verb (v) is not the first element of the sentence, e.g. because a time phrase comes first, then it has to go after the verb.
Wir (s) beginnen (v) um neun Uhr.
Um neun Uhr beginnen (v) wir (s).
Ich (s) gehe (v) am Abend nach Hause.
Am Abend gehe (v) ich (s) nach Hause.   **G21**

Auf Deutsch

KLIMAWANDEL

Risiko für die Natur
EUROPÄISCHE KONFERENZ 17. – 19. April

7 **1•22** Later, Martin tells Ricardo about the first day of the conference. Listen, then fill the gaps with the times mentioned. Use the vocabulary in the box to help you understand.

.... beginnen wir mit dem Vortrag des Ministers zum Klimawandel. .... treffen wir die anderen europäischen Delegierten und dann diskutieren wir das Thema Klimawandel. ....machen wir eine Kaffeepause, und dann sprechen wir mit dem Minister bis zum Mittagessen ....

Nach dem Mittagessen besichtigen wir eine Firma für Umwelttechnik. .... gehen alle Delegierten in ein Restaurant und .... essen wir zusammen zu Abend.

der Vortrag *lecture*	**treffen** *to meet*	**der Klimawandel** *climate change*
besichtigen *to visit*	**die Umwelt(technik)** *environment (technology)*	

Talking about daily routine

1   1•23 Listen to the key language:

Ich wache/stehe ... auf	I wake/get up ...
früh	early
normalerweise/manchmal	usually/sometimes
so gegen zehn Uhr	around ten o'clock
Ich trainiere im Fitnessstudio.	I work out/train in the gym.
Ich dusche mich.	I have a shower.
Ich ziehe mich an.	I get dressed.
Ich entspanne mich.	I relax.
Ich gehe ins Bett.	I go to bed.

2   1•24 Listen to six people talking about their morning routine, and match the times with the activities.

a	06.10	**1**	sich duschen
b	08.00	**2**	aufstehen
c	08.15	**3**	sich entspannen
d	08.30	**4**	aufwachen
e	23.00	**5**	im Fitnessstudio trainieren
f	06.45	**6**	sich anziehen

Auf Deutsch

The infinitive of some verbs is followed by **sich** *oneself*, which is rarely translated into English, e.g. **sich duschen** *to shower (oneself)*. Sich changes according to the subject of the verb: **ich dusche mich** *I shower (myself)*.

ich dusche mich	**wir duschen uns**
du duschst dich	**ihr duscht euch**
er/sie/es duscht sich	**sie/Sie duschen sich** G16–17

3   1•25 Listen to Martin telling Ricardo about his daily routine. He refers to what he does **nach der Arbeit**. **Nach** means *after*, as well as *to* (a place) and *past* (the hour). See if you can catch:
- what time he normally gets up;
- what two things he does before work;
- what he sometimes does after work – and where he does it;
- what he does after this.

Now say what time you normally wake up and get up.

... and the working day

4 1•26 Listen to the key language:

Um wieviel Uhr ...?	What time ...?
Er pendelt.	He commutes.
Er verlässt das Haus.	He leaves the house.
Er geht ins Fitnessstudio.	He goes to the gym.
Ich sehe fern. (from **fernsehen**)	I watch TV.

5 1•27 Listen as Martin's wife Anja talks about their routine. Decide whether these statements apply to Martin or Anja or to both of them. You will notice that the verb **pendeln** loses its **e** in the **ich** form. This is common to all verbs ending in **-eln** in the infinitive.

		Martin	Anja
a	Ich stehe um sieben Uhr auf.		
b	Ich arbeite von zuhause.		
c	Ich dusche mich um halb neun.		
d	Ich pendle.		
e	Ich verlasse das Haus um 07.25.		
f	Ich gehe am Abend ins Fitnessstudio.		
g	Ich esse um Viertel nach acht zu Abend.		
h	Ich sehe fern.		

Not all verbs follow the **wohnen** pattern of regular endings. Those that don't, such as **sprechen** to talk, **essen** to eat and **verlassen** to leave are called irregular verbs, and the majority of them differ from **wohnen** only in their **du** and **er/sie/es** endings. However, a few, such as **haben** to have and **sein** to be, are wholly irregular. **G20**

	verlassen	sprechen	essen	haben	sein
ich	verlasse	spreche	esse	habe	bin
du	verlässt	sprichst	isst	hast	bist
er/sie/es	verlässt	spricht	isst	hat	ist
wir	verlassen	sprechen	essen	haben	sind
ihr	verlasst	sprecht	esst	habt	seid
sie/Sie	verlassen	sprechen	essen	haben	sind

Auf Deutsch

6 Can you:
- ask a friend what time he/she wakes up/gets up?
- say what time someone you know wakes up/gets up?
- say these things about yourself and another person, using *we*?

put it all together

1 Find a connection between the words in the two columns.

a	ins Bett gehen	1	Vortrag
b	trainieren	2	Pause
c	verlassen	3	T-Shirt
d	aufwachen	4	am Abend
e	Kaffee	5	Fitnessstudio
f	Konferenz	6	morgens
g	sich anziehen	7	Haus

2 Write the following in German, in 12-hour clock format, like the example.

a at **20.00** um acht Uhr abends

b at **20.00** ....

c at **16.15** ....

d at **06.20** ....

e at **23.00** ....

3 Fill the gaps with the right form of the verb in brackets.

a Dietmar ist Architekt und ...... in Bremen. (arbeiten)

b Die Konferenz ...... nicht früh. (beginnen)

c Meine Frau und ich ...... von zuhause. (arbeiten)

d Am Samstag ...... wir um halb zehn ...... (aufstehen)

e Nach der Arbeit ...... ich im Fitnessstudio. (trainieren)

f Ich ...... um sieben Uhr ...... (aufstehen), dann ...... ich ......
(sich duschen) und ich ...... mich ...... (sich anziehen).

4 How would you tell someone in German that you:
- normally wake up early;
- then (**dann**) get up at 7.30;
- leave the house at eight o'clock;
- commute;
- go home at seven o'clock in the evening;
- watch television;
- have supper;
- sometimes go to bed at 11 o' clock?

1 **1●28** Answer these questions as if you were Michael Taylor from the North West of England.

- **Michael, wo wohnst du?**
- ◆ Say you live in Cheshire.
- **Aber du arbeitest in Manchester, nicht wahr?**
- ◆ Say yes, you commute.
- **Um wieviel Uhr stehst du normalerweise auf?**
- ◆ Say you normally wake up at seven o'clock and get up at ten past.
- **Und um wieviel Uhr verlässt du das Haus?**
- ◆ Say you leave the house at half past seven.

2 **1●29** Now answer the questions as if you were Michael's wife, Sandra.

- **Sandra, um wieviel Uhr steht Michael auf?**
- ◆ Say he gets up at ten past seven.
- **Wo arbeitet er?**
- ◆ Say he works in Manchester and leaves the house at half past seven.
- **Sandra, gehst du ins Fitnessstudio?**
- ◆ Say yes, you go to the gym sometimes.
- **Esst ihr zusammen zu Abend?**
- ◆ **Zusammen** means *together*. Say yes, you eat your evening meal together.
- **Um wieviel Uhr esst ihr zu Abend?**
- ◆ Say you usually eat at seven in the evening.
- **Und um wieviel Uhr entspannt ihr euch?**
- ◆ Say you relax at ten o'clock. Normally, you and Michael watch TV together.

quiz

1 What time is **zwanzig Minuten vor vier nachmittags?**

2 **Spät** is the opposite of **früh**; what does it mean in English?

3 What's **Klimawandel?**

4 Add **sechzig** and **zwölf**. What's the answer in German?

5 Is it **mich**, **sich** or **uns** that's missing here? Ich **dusche ...... um sieben Uhr.**

6 How would you say *We leave the house at half past five and arrive at seven o'clock?*

7 *Marta commutes* is **Marta ......**

8 When you hear **Es tut mir leid**, do you expect good news or bad?

Now check whether you can ...

- understand and say times using both the 12- and 24-hour clock
- say what happens when
- say *we* do something if you're given the infinitive of a verb
- talk about your daily routine
- describe people's work routine

This first section of *Talk German 2* has been about revisiting the basics as well as extending your German. There's more consolidation to come in **Noch mehr!** but, if you're finding at this stage that some of what you learnt previously has escaped your memory, now would be a good time to look back and remind yourself of key basics: numbers and vocabulary such as the months and days of the week (see page 131). It can be quite therapeutic to go over something familiar that you learnt very early on.

Noch mehr! 1

References to time, manner and place go in that order within a sentence, with more general information going before the specific.

Ich fahre <u>seit Januar</u> (T1) <u>jeden Tag</u> (T2) <u>langsam</u> (M1) <u>mit dem Fahrrad</u> by bike (M2) <u>nach Regensburg</u> (P1) <u>zur Arbeit</u> (P2).

G21

1 Simona and Michael, friends who haven't met for years, bump into each other. Simona has a lot of questions for Michael – but his replies are jumbled up. Rearrange each one in two possible ways, starting with 1 the subject, 2 the timing.

a **S** Wo wohnst du jetzt?
   M wohne/seit fast drei Monaten/hier in München/ich/in der Nymphenburger Straße

b **S** Und wo wohnt deine Schwester jetzt?
   M in Mannheim/wohnen/seit 2010/meine Schwester und ihr Mann

c **S** Arbeitet Stefan immer noch *still* an der Kunsthalle in Mannheim?
   M studiert/seit zwei Jahren/an der Heidelberger Universität/ Stefan

d **S** Ist Stefan verheiratet?
   M mit Sylvia/seit vier Monaten/ist/er/verheiratet

e **S** Und bist du verheiratet?
   M verheiratet/mit Elisabeth/seit acht Jahren/bin/ich

f **S** Wo arbeitest du?
   M pendle/nach Augsburg/seit zwei Monaten/jeden Tag/ich

-n is added to a plural noun after **seit** *for/since*:

| das Jahr | die Jahre (pl) | seit zwei Jahren |
| der Tag | die Tage (pl) | seit fünf Tagen |

In grammatical terms, this is because **seit** is followed by the dative case.

G4

2 These pictures show Michael's daily routine. Make sentences saying
what he does and when, starting with the time. The infinitives of the
verbs you need are in the box. Example: **Um 5.15 wacht er auf**.

a   5.15   b   5.30   c   5.45   d   6.00

e   7.00   f   8.00-17.00   g   19.00   h   20.00-23.00

> sich duschen   nach Hause kommen   sich anziehen   aufwachen
> arbeiten   sich entspannen   aufstehen   das Haus verlassen

3 Using the 12-hour clock, how would you tell a visitor to the UK what
time banks and shops usually open and close?

In	öffnen	die Banken	um
Großbritannien	schließen	die Geschäfte	

?

4 Read what people say about why they do certain things. Join the two
sentences using **weil**, bearing in mind that the first verb in the **weil**
clause must go at the end and that in German a comma separates the
two clauses, e.g:

Ich gehe ins Fitnessstudio. Ich trainiere gern.
Ich gehe ins Fitnessstudio, weil ich gern trainiere.

a   Mein Bruder wohnt in Deutschland. Er arbeitet bei Lufthansa.
b   Ich lerne Deutsch. Ich mag Deutschland.
c   Sie spricht Englisch. Sie wohnt in England.
d   Sie lernen Deutsch. Sie möchten in Österreich arbeiten.
e   Er steht früh auf. Die Arbeit beginnt um sieben Uhr morgens.

5 Using the adverb **gern**, how would you say you like:

a   travelling   b   training in the gym
c   commuting   d   learning German
e   watching TV

6   Without using the glossary, read what nine-year-old Max produced in school when asked to write about his family. **Leben** means *to live*.

> Meine Familie von Max Brosius
>
> Darf ich meine Familie vorstellen?
>
> Mein Urgroßvater heißt Josef Brosius und ist achtzig Jahre alt. Er kommt aus der Schweiz. Er ist 1932, also noch vor dem Zweiten Weltkrieg, geboren und ist sehr, sehr alt. Er ist Witwer und lebt alleine.
>
> Sein Sohn Robert ist mein Großvater. Er ist auch alt. Er ist mit meiner Großmutter Luise verheiratet. Sie hat fünf Schwestern. Arme Großmutter! Ich habe nur EINE Schwester! Sie ist vier Jahre alt und heißt Lili. Meine Großeltern wohnen in der Schweiz und haben drei Kinder, zwei Söhne und eine Tochter. Mein Onkel Dietmar arbeitet seit vielen Jahren in Brasilien. Ich glaube, er ist Bankier. Seine Frau ist Portugiesin. Ich habe drei Cousins in Brasilien. Sie wohnen in einem großen Haus in São Paulo.
>
> Mein Vater heißt Holger und ist mit meiner Mutter verheiratet. Meine Mutter heißt Karin Borchert. Ihre Mutter, Oma Johanna, kommt aus Niedersachsen in Norddeutschland, aber wohnt jetzt in Jena. Manchmal fahren wir nach Jena.
>
> Meine Tante Renate wohnt weit weg. Seit 2005 wohnt sie mit meinem Onkel Rolf und meinen Cousinen in Amerika. Sie heißen Michaela und Claudia. Ich mag Claudia nicht!

Choose the right option. (You may need to use the glossary).

a Dietmar ist der Großvater/Vater/Bruder/Schwager von Karin.

b Johanna ist die Schwester/Mutter/Kusine/Schwiegermutter von Holger.

c Max ist der Sohn/Bruder/Cousin/Enkel von Robert.

d Max hat drei/vier/fünf/sechs Cousins und Kusinen.

e Der Schwiegervater von Luise heißt Robert/Max/Josef/Holger.

f Der Vater von Dietmar heißt Robert/Max/Josef/Holger.

g Die Eltern von Holger haben zwei/drei/vier/fünf Kinder.

h Michaela und Claudia sind Kusinen/Tanten/Schwestern/Großmütter.

7   Ricardo Silva is a **Wissenschaftler** *scientist* attending the **Klimawandel** conference in Berlin. He is **Portugiese** *Portuguese*.

  a   Write down what he might say, based on this information:

> **Surname:** Silva   **First name:** Ricardo
> **Nationality:** Portuguese
> **Works in:** Lisbon
> **Profession:** Scientist; has worked for Greenpeace since 2001
> **Languages spoken:** Portuguese (**Portugiesisch**), German, English

  b   After the conference, a few delegates meet informally. Write down how Ricardo would tell them he:

  - lives in Cascais in Portugal and commutes to work;
  - has been married for two years and has two children;
  - really likes travelling and would like to work in Brazil.

Auf Deutsch

'Case' refers to the different roles that a noun or pronoun can play in a sentence. It can be:

Nominative: the subject of the sentence, carrying out the verb;

Accusative: the direct object of the verb, directly affected by it;

Dative: the indirect object of the verb, affected by it but indirectly;

Genitive: relating to possession.

Case affects not only the ending of the noun itself but also words used with it, such as articles and adjectives.

Der junge Mann (nominative) **lernt Portugiesisch.**

Sie mag den junge Mann (accusative).

Sie gibt dem jungen Mann (dative) **einen guten Laptop** (accusative).

Der Name (nominative) **des jungen Mannes** (genitive) **ist Hans.**

G4

Kann ich hier buchen?

talking about leisure interests

getting local information

asking for advice

planning an activity

In Deutschland ...

not only are there many historic and artistic treasures, but there are also 14 **Nationalparks** and over 8,400 **Naturschutzgebiete** *nature reserves*.

The **Deutsche Zentrale für Tourismus (DZT)** *German National Tourist Board* provides information online and in the local tourist office (**Fremdenverkehrsamt**) about things to see and do. These may range from the world-famous **Oktoberfest** *beer festival* in Munich to regional **Winzerfeste** *wine festivals* and **Sport**, including **Extremsport**. And, with 70,000 kilometres of **Radwege** *cycle paths* and 350 **Heil-und Kurorte** *spa resorts*, there's plenty to do.

Talking about leisure interests

1 **1•30** Listen to the key language:

Was machst du normalerweise am Wochenende?	What do you normally do at the weekend?
Ich mache lieber Kung Fu.	I prefer kung fu.
Am liebsten windsurfe ich.	I like windsurfing best.
Interessierst du dich für Sport?	Are you interested in sport?
Mir gefallen alle Kampfsportarten.	I like all types of martial arts.

2 **1•31** Listen as Lukas, Silke and Elke talk about what they like to do, and make a note of their interests. The vocabulary below will help you.

 Fußball spielen   **Windsurfen**

 Kung Fu machen   **wandern gehen**   **schwimmen**

> **Gefällt** is often used to talk about what you like doing: **Mir gefällt die Natur** I like nature. (**Mir** here is the dative case of **ich** (to me).) Because this literally means *Nature is pleasing to me*, you need the plural **gefallen** *are pleasing* to talk about liking something plural: **Mir gefallen Filme** I like films. When saying what other people like, you replace **mir** to me with the appropriate pronoun: **Uns gefallen Filme** We like films (for a complete list see page 136).

3 **1•32** Read the following, then listen to Elke's father talking about the family's interest in trekking. Tick the phrases as you hear them.

lange Spaziergänge *long walks*
entdecken gerne idyllische Dörfer *discover idyllic villages*
bewundern gern das Panorama *admire the panoramic view*
genießen die Stille *enjoy the peace and quiet*

4 Have a go at talking about your interests – your own and any that you share with other people.

Getting local information

5 1•33 Listen to the key language:

Kann ich Ihnen helfen?	Can I help you?
Wann öffnet ...?	When does ... open?
Gibt es hier in der Nähe ...?	Is/Are there ... round here?
Es gibt viele.	There are many (of them).
Muss man ... reservieren?	Do you have to reserve ...?
Wenn Sie möchten, ...	If you would like ...

6 **Touristeninformation** publications such as the following are freely available in German tourist offices. See if you can work out what these are: many of the words are similar to English so only use the glossary if you're really stuck.

der Restaurantführer

der Hotelführer

der Gastronomie- und Weinführer

die Karte der Region

die Liste der Führungen

die Liste der Museumsöffnungszeiten

der Stadtplan

der Veranstaltungs- und Messekalender

der Sport- und Erlebnisführer

die Liste der Campingplätze

Können *to be able to* and **müssen** *to have to* are irregular and are followed by a second verb in the infinitive: **ich singe** *I sing*; **ich kann singen** *I can sing*; **ich muss singen** *I must sing*.
The second verb goes at the end of the clause:

Wir können eine Führung <u>reservieren</u>.

G15

Auf Deutsch

---

7 1•34 Listen to people making enquiries at the **Touristeninformation**. Which of the above publications are mentioned? You'll hear **gratis** *free* and **Broschüre** *brochure*.

Listen again and note the different forms of **ein** in the replies: **Wir haben einen** (m) **Stadtplan/eine Broschüre** (f)/**ein Informationsblatt** (n) *information sheet*. These are the accusative case endings, which have to be used after **haben**.

Asking for advice

1 **1•35** Listen to the key language:

Was kann man hier machen/sehen?	What is there to do/see? (Lit. What can one do/see here?)
Wenn Sie sich für ... interessieren, ...	If you're interested in ...
Wenn Sie lieber ... erkunden, ...	If you'd rather explore ...
Das sollten Sie nicht verpassen.	You shouldn't miss that.

2 **1•36** As you listen to more tourists making enquiries at the **Fremdenverkehrsamt** tick the following when you hear them.

mit dem Auto

mit dem Fahrrad

eine Naturlehrwanderung

das Schloss

das Winzerfest

das Weingut

das Vogelschutzgebiet

Auf Deutsch

Within clauses that are dependent on the main clause, e.g. starting with **weil** *because* or **wenn** *if, whenever*, the verb goes to the end: **Weil ich Deutschland <u>liebe</u>! Wenn Sie gerne <u>wandern</u>** ... If the **wenn** clause starts the sentence, the next clause begins with the verb, followed by the subject:

Wenn Sie gerne wandern, <u>können Sie</u> eine Naturlehrwanderung reservieren.

G21

---

3 Now read the conversation and fill the gaps.

Was ...... man hier in der Gegend machen?
Also, wenn Sie gerne wandern, ... Sie eine Naturlehrwanderung im Nationalpark machen. Wenn Sie lieber die Gegend mit dem Auto – oder mit dem Fahrrad – erkunden, gibt es hier viel zu .... Es gibt hier das Vogelschutzgebiet oder Sie können auch zum Weingut .... Oder wenn Sie sich für Kultur und Tradition ......, gibt es das Wieslocher Winzerfest. Das sollten Sie nicht ......!

Planning an activity

4 **1•37** Listen to the key language:

Kann man ...?	Can one/you ...?
Darf man ...?	Is one/Are you allowed ...?
Man sollte ...	One/you should ...
Man muss ...	One/you must ...
Gibt es eine Ermäßigung?	Is there a discount?

> **Man** is used in German where English uses *one, we,* or *you* in a non-specific sense: **Man muss im voraus reservieren** *You must reserve in advance*; **Kann man mit Kreditkarte bezahlen?** *Can one/ we pay by credit card?* It has the same verb endings as **er, sie** and **es.**

5 **1•38** At the **Fremdenverkehrsamt**, someone wants to book a guided walk in the Nature Reserve: **Ich interessiere mich für die Führung durch das Naturschutzgebiet. Kann ich die Führung hier buchen?** Listen a couple of times and identify from this list what was <u>not</u> mentioned. Then read the transcript on page 111.

- You don't need to book.
- There's a walk every day.
- It starts at 09.00.
- It lasts (**sie dauert**) four hours.
- You must bring food and water.
- You must wear sturdy shoes.
- You should bring a sweater/ sweatshirt.

6 **1•39** Matthias and a friend decide to **mieten** *hire* bikes **morgen** *tomorrow*. Listen as he rings the hire company and note:

- how long they want the bikes for;
- how much it costs per bike;
- how much discount Matthias's offered.

Fahrradverleih	**Ausweispapiere erforderlich**
Leihgebühren	- *Ausweis oder Pass*
1 Stunde €5	- *Kreditkarte (Kaution €300)*
1 Tag €15	**Zubehör**
Ermäßigung	*Helm*
15% pro Gruppe mit mindestens 5 Fahrrädern	*Fahrradschloss*

put it all together

1 Match the two halves.

a	Mir gefällt	1	feste Schuhe tragen.
b	Kann ich	2	mit Kreditkarte bezahlen?
c	Haben Sie	3	Ermäßigungen für Gruppen
d	Ich interessiere mich für die	4	die Natur
e	Es gibt	5	einen Stadtplan?
f	Man muss	6	alle Extremsportarten.
g	Mir gefallen	7	Naturlehrwanderung durch den Park.

2 What words are missing from the gaps?

    a Interessierst du .... für Film?
    b .... gefällt Fotografieren.
    c Ich interessiere .... für die deutsche Sprache.
    d Herr Schlosser, gefallen ..... alle Sportarten?

3 Your neighbour's granddaughter has just received an e-mail from a new penfriend in Germany and can't read it. Explain to her what this extract says, using the glossary for any new words.

> Ich habe nicht viele Hobbys. Ich gehe gerne mit meinen Freunden aus. Ich gehe auch gern mit meinen Freunden in die Stadt und einkaufen. Wir gehen besonders gern ins Sportzentrum, wo wir Federball und Handball spielen. Ich spiele gern Federball, aber ich spiele lieber Tischtennis. Man kann dort auch Squash spielen, aber ich bin nicht so gut in Squash. Am liebsten spiele ich Tennis – im Sommer spiele ich jeden Tag mit meiner Schwester.
>
> Ich interessiere mich auch sehr für Fotografie. Ich fotografiere oft – am liebsten fotografiere ich die Natur.
>
> Mir gefällt Musik, weil meine Tante Sängerin ist. Und ich tanze auch gern – ich habe jeden Mittwoch Tanzstunden. Was machst du gerne in deiner Freizeit? Interessiert du dich auch für Fotografie?

now you're talking!

1 **1•40** Imagine you're at the tourist office in Bremen. You're with a friend, so you'll be using *we*.

● **Guten Tag. Kann ich Ihnen helfen?**
◆ Greet her and ask if they have a food and wine guide.
● **Ja, bitte. Hier finden Sie alle Restaurants und Gaststätten.**
◆ Ask if there's a restaurant nearby.
● **Wenn Sie gerne deutsche Küche essen, gibt es das Haus Meier. Es hat einen guten Ruf.**
◆ Now ask what there is to do in Bremen.
● **Also, es gibt hier viel zu sehen und zu machen. Ich gebe Ihnen diesen Stadtführer und diesen Veranstaltungskalender.**
◆ Say you're interested in nature. Ask if you can go on a guided tour (lit. *make a guided tour*) in the National Park (**im Nationalpark**).
● **Im Nationalpark Harz gibt es Führungen zu Fuß, zu Pferd oder mit dem Mountainbike. Hier sind ein paar Informationen. Sie können im voraus buchen .... Sie müssen auch bequeme Schuhe tragen!**
◆ You also want transport. Ask if you can hire a bike nearby.
● **Ja, in der Steilstraße ... Hier ist ein Stadtplan ... die Steilstraße ist hier.**

2 **1•41** You're chatting to Armin, who you've met on holiday. He's just suggested **Sollen wir uns duzen?**

◆ Ask him what he does at the weekend.
● **Also, ich gehe einkaufen, gehe mit meinen Freunden aus – wir gehen ins Kino, in die Disko ... und wir gehen zusammen essen.**
◆ Ask him if he's interested in sport.
● **Ja, ich interessiere mich für Sport. Ich spiele gern Volleyball. Mir gefällt auch Tischtennis.**
◆ Ask him if he's interested in football.
● **Fußball? Aber natürlich – ich bin Schalke 04-Fan. Aber sag mal, was machst du in deiner Freizeit?**

3 Using the glossary, tell an English-speaking friend what Armin does at the weekend.

quiz

1 What does **die Karte der Region** refer to?

2 Would you use **können** or **kann** after **man**?

3 To ask a group of people you have just met if they're interested in football, would you use **interessierst du dich**, **interessiert sie sich** or **interessieren Sie sich**?

4 What should you make sure you have when you see the sign **Ausweispapiere erforderlich:** your cycling helmet, your passport or other ID, or your map?

5 What do **kann**, **ist** and **hat** have in common?

6 **Stadtführer**, **Liste**, **Broschüre**, **Karte**, **Ermäßigung**. Which is the odd one out and why?

7 What is the difference between **Muss man mit Kreditkarte bezahlen?** and **Darf man mit Kreditkarte bezahlen?**

8 What does **Das sollte man nicht verpassen!** mean?

Now check whether you can ...

- ask for information and advice in a tourist office
- ask about/say what you and other people can do
- arrange an activity
- talk about what you like to do in your spare time
- ask others about their leisure interests

If you access **www.germany.travel/en/**, the official website of the German Tourist Board, you'll find it full of fascinating facts and figures about Germany. You can change the language setting for information in German about leisure activities, culture and towns. Try to skim read, i.e. don't get hung up on single words that you don't understand but try to get the flow of the passage. If you then reset the language, you'll find the same information in English and you can compare the two.

Was hältst du von dieser Jacke?

shopping for clothes

... and shoes and bags

expressing your opinion

making comparisons

In Deutschland ...

Design and **Mode** *fashion* play an important role in everyday life. Fashion labels and designers such as Boss, Lagerfeld and Joop have become household names worldwide. Fashion capitals such as Berlin, Hamburg and Düsseldorf make shopping for clothes and accessories a pleasurable experience.

A lot of English words in the **Modeindustrie** have settled into German patterns. Many of these are neuter: **das Top**, **das T-Shirt**, **das Sweatshirt**, but there are exceptions too: **die Jeans** (feminine or plural), **der Pullover**.

Shopping for clothes

1 **1•42** Listen to the key language:

Ich suche ...	I'm looking for ...
ein Top/ein weißes Hemd	a top/a white shirt
eine Jacke/eine graue Hose	a jacket/a pair of grey trousers
einen grünen Pullover aus Wolle	a green wool jumper
Welche Größe haben Sie?	What size are you?
Ich sehe mich nur um.	I'm just browsing.

2 **1•43** Get familiar with the words below, listen to some conversations heard in clothes shops and note in English what people are buying.

> **weiß** *white*   **schwarz** *black*   **grau** *grey*   **grün** *green*
> **rot** *red*   **gelb** *yellow*   **blau** *blue*   **hellblau** *light blue*
> **dunkelblau** *dark blue*   **Baumwolle** *cotton*   **Wolle** *wool*
> **Leinen** *linen* **Seide** *silk*   **Kaschmir** *cashmere*

	a	b	c	d	e	f
Farbe *colour*						
Stoff *material*						
Größe *size*						

Auf Deutsch

Adjectives after a noun + **sein** *to be* are always in the dictionary form. But an adjective <u>before</u> a noun adds an ending, which agrees in gender, number and case with that noun. Some of the endings are slightly different after the definite and indefinite articles.

	masculine	feminine	neuter
nom.	der blaue/ein blauer Pullover	die blaue/eine blaue Jacke	das blaue/ein blaues Hemd
acc.	den blauen/einen blauen Pullover	die blaue/eine blaue Jacke	das blaue/ein blaues Hemd

G6

3 **1•44** Listen to a couple out shopping for clothes then answer these questions:
  a What are they looking for?   **b** What colours do they ask for?
  c Who is it for?   **d** What do they decide on?

... and shoes and bags

4 **1•45** Listen to the key language:

Ich möchte … anprobieren.	I'd like to try … on.
Möchten Sie sie anprobieren?	Would you like to try them on?
Kann ich mal sehen?	Can I have a look?
Ich möchte ihn umtauschen.	I'd like to exchange it (m).

There are several words for *it* depending on gender and case.

	m	f	n	
nom.	er	sie	es	
acc.	ihn	sie	es	*Them* is sie.

G11

5 **1•46** In a shoe shop a customer has seen some **Stiefel** *boots* she likes and wants to try them on. Listen and jot down:

a what size she takes: ....
b what sizes they have in stock: ....
c what other colour she's offered: ....

6 Using the glossary, read this advert for **ein Rucksack** *a backpack*.

> **Leichter Sportrucksack** aus wasserfestem Stoff. Waschbar. Komfortabel und geräumig; vorderes Fach mit verstärktem Reißverschluss, zwei Seitentaschen (eine Seitentasche mit Reißverschluss); Handy-Fach

a Underline the adjectives used to describe the backpack.
b What's the German for i) zip, ii) pocket and iii) side pockets?

7 **1•47** A customer saying **Ich habe diesen Rucksack gekauft** *I bought this backpack* has brought it back to the shop because something is **defekt** *broken*. Listen and:

a note in English what's wrong;
b note in German the words he uses to say he wants to change it.

Expressing your opinion

1 **1•48** Listen to the key language:

Was hältst du von ...?	What do you think of ...?
Steht sie mir?	Does it suit me?
Ich glaube, ...	I think ...
er/sie/es ist zu lang.	it's too long.
sie sind zu kurz.	they are too short.
Dieser/diese/dieses steht dir besser.	That one suits you better.

2 **1•49** Dietmar's mother and sister are helping him choose clothes for his wedding. Listen and tick the items as you hear them.

dieses Hemd   **diese Krawatte**   **diese Weste**   **diese Jacke**

diese Hose   **diese Schuhe**   **diese Fliege**

Dies- plus the appropriate ending means *this* and *that*. **Hier** or **da** can be added for clarification. The endings are the same for **welch-?** *which?*: **Welches Hemd** (n)? – **Dieses hier.**

	m	f	n	pl
nom.	dieser	diese	dieses	diese
acc.	diesen	diese	dieses	diese
dat.	diesem	dieser	diesem	diesen

G10

3 **1•49** Listen again and insert the right form of **dies-**. Check your answers with the full dialogue on page 113.

a Mutti, was hältst du von (dat.) ...... Jacke?

b Ich glaube, ... hier steht dir besser.

c Ach nein, Susanne! .... da ist zu bunt *bright*. Mutti, ... Hose hier – ist sie zu lang?

d Nein, sie ist perfekt. Und dazu *with it* ...... schwarzen Schuhe. Was hältst du von (dat.) ...... Krawatte?

e Na ja, ... da ist etwas blass *pale*!

f Mir gefällt ..... Fliege.

Making comparisons

4 1•50 Listen to the key language:

Welches Kleid gefällt Ihnen besser?	Which dress do you like better?
Mir gefällt das gelbe besser als das rote.	I like the yellow one better than the red one.
Das rote ist etwas bequemer.	The red one is a bit more comfortable.
Das gelbe ist nicht so teuer wie das rote.	The yellow one is not as expensive as the red one.
Das stimmt.	That's correct.

> To compare things, you add -er to the adjective: **eleganter** *more elegant. Than* is *als*: **Das T-Shirt ist enger** *tighter* **als der Pullover.** An umlaut is added to the **a**, **o** or **u** of a short adjective: **lang** *long*, **länger** *longer*. Adjectives already ending in -er drop the e: **teuer** *expensive*, **teurer** *more expensive*.
>
> **G8**

Auf Deutsch

5 1•51 Gerda's found two dresses and she and Susanne are discussing them while the **Verkäuferin** *shop assistant* hovers. Listen then summarise in English what Gerda thinks of each dress.

Verkäuferin:	**Welches Kleid gefällt Ihnen besser?**
Gerda:	**Das rote ist praktischer.**
Susanne:	**Mir gefällt das gelbe besser als das rote. Es ist modischer** *more fashionable.*
Gerda:	**Das gelbe ist etwas enger, aber das rote ist etwas bequemer.**
Susanne:	**Mutti, ich glaube, das rote ist ein bisschen kurz für dich.**
Gerda:	**Das stimmt, das gelbe ist länger. Das gelbe ist besser – es ist nicht so teuer wie das rote.**

6 1•52 Gerda tries on one more dress, which Susanne and the shop assistant feel very differently about. Listen and pick out the adjectives used to describe it. If you need help, the transcript is on page 114.

put it all together

1 What's the opposite of these (in German)?

   a schwarz   b kurz
   c blass   d klein
   e altmodisch   f unpraktisch
   g billig *cheap*

2 Fill the gaps with the appropriate adjective. Remember
   that the position of the adjective in the sentence influences
   whether or not it has an ending.

   a Steht mir diese .... Jacke?
   b Die Krawatte ist sehr .....
   c Gefallen dir die .... Schuhe?
   d Sind die Stiefel etwas .....?
   e Ich möchte einen .... Pullover.
   f Mein neuer Rucksack ist sehr .....

   > **langärmeligen**
   > *long sleeved*
   > **weiße**
   > **schwarzen**
   > **bunt**
   > **geräumig**
   > **groß**

3 Rewrite these sentences, replacing the
   shaded words with *it* or *them*. The verb **bezahlen** means *to
   pay* or *to pay for* depending on the context.

   a Ich kaufe meine Kleider in Düsseldorf.
   b Ich wasche dieses Hemd von Hand.
   c Kann ich diesen Rucksack umtauschen?
   d Ich möchte die schwarzen Stiefel bezahlen.
   e Bezahlen Sie diese Jacke mit Kreditkarte?
   f Ich möchte die blauen Schuhe anprobieren.

4 How would you say you're looking for:

   a jeans in size 38;
   b a white linen shirt;
   c a dark blue pure wool jacket, size 40;
   d a lightweight, waterproof rucksack?

now you're talking!

1   **1•53** You're out shopping for clothes.

- **Kann ich Ihnen helfen?**
- ◆ Say you're looking for a jacket.
- **Welche Größe haben Sie?**
- ◆ You're a 46.
- **Also. Wir haben Jacken aus Baumwolle, Leinen, Jeans … oder möchten Sie vielleicht eine Jacke aus Wolle?**
- ◆ Say yes, you'd like a wool jacket.
- **Welche Farbe?**
- ◆ You're not entirely sure. Say black or dark blue.
- **Wir haben diese in dunkelblau aus reiner Wolle oder diese hier aus Wolle mit vierzig Prozent Kaschmir.**
- ◆ Ask if you can try the black one on.
- **Ja, bitte – diese hier ist sehr schön.**
- ◆ Ask how much it costs.
- **Sie ist sehr billig – nur €390!**

2   **1•54** On to another shop to change a wallet (**eine Brieftasche**).

- **Gibt es ein Problem?**
- ◆ Say yes, this wallet is broken and you'd like to change it.
- **Kann ich mal sehen? Wo ist sie defekt?**
- ◆ Point to the broken fastening and say *here*.
- **Leider haben wir keine anderen in dieser Art. Gefällt Ihnen diese hier?**
- ◆ Ask your friend what she thinks of this (one).
- **Ich glaube, sie ist ein bisschen klein.**

3   **1•55** To a third shop, where your friend tries on a pair of boots which are **im Angebot** *on offer*.

- **Gefallen sie dir? Stehen sie mir?**
- ◆ She's asking whether they suit her – and you think they're hideous. Say that in your opinion they're a bit tight.
- **Aber sie sind so schön … und sie sind im Angebot!**
- ◆ You find a different pair and tell her you like these better (**… gefallen … besser**) and they're cheaper.
- **Toll! Sie sind fantastisch!**

quiz

1 In a shop, how would you say you're just browsing?

2 How would you say what you're looking for?

3 You've just tried on some nice shoes, and they're a perfect fit. You hear **Sind sie zu eng?** – what are you being asked?

4 What colour do you think **sonnengelb** is?

5 Referring to a jacket, how would you say you like the grey one?

6 **Das Hemd ist teurer ...... die Jacke**. What's the missing word?

7 You see a jacket you like and want to say that you'd like to try this one on. What would you say?

8 What's the German for a zip?

Now check whether you can ...

- say what you're looking for in a shop
- use adjectives to describe something
- express your opinion and ask for someone else's
- compare things using adjective + -**er** and **als**
- use the correct forms of *this*
- use *it* and *them* in the correct form
- express a preference

Being able to give an opinion in a new language is a great step forward. Get used to saying in German what you think: comment on the news using **ich glaube** and adjectives such as **herrlich** *splendid*, **tragisch**, **lächerlich** *ridiculous* or **wunderbar**.

Try commenting on the contents of your wardrobe: describing clothes as **neu** *new*, **alt** *old* or even **altmodisch**, comparing them using -**er** and **nicht so**, and perhaps evaluating them as **ideal** or **perfekt** or **eine Katastrophe!**

Noch mehr! 2

1 Read these snippets of information about four of Germany's 16 **Bundesländer** *federal states*. See if you can work out where they are and match them to the numbers on the map.

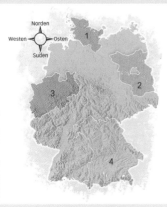

a ..... liegt in Westdeutschland und hat über 17,5 Millionen Einwohner. Im nördlichen Teil befindet sich das Ruhrgebiet. Das Ruhrgebiet ist eine der größten Metropolregionen der Welt. Köln ist die Stadt mit den meisten Einwohnern im Bundesland. Hier kann man den Kölner Dom finden. Die Landeshauptstadt ist Düsseldorf.

b ..... ist das größte Bundesland und liegt im Südosten von Deutschland neben der Tschechischen Republik und Österreich. Man findet dort die Alpen und das Mittelgebirge. Der höchste Punkt ist der Gipfel der Zugspitze auf einer Höhe von 2,962 Metern. Die Landeshauptstadt München ist bekannt für das Oktoberfest.

c .... ist das nördlichste Land Deutschlands und liegt zwischen der Ostsee und der Nordsee und grenzt im Norden an Dänemark. Das Land ist bekannt für seinen Nationalpark. Der Nationalpark Wattenmeer ist der größte in Mitteleuropa. Die Küste ist ideal für Wassersportarten wie Angeln, Segeln und Surfen.

d .... liegt im Osten von Deutschland und grenzt an Polen. Seine Hauptstadt ist Potsdam. Hier gibt es ungefähr 800 Seen, was es sehr attraktiv für den Tourismus macht. Man findet hier auch den Nationalpark Unteres Odertal. Besonders sehenswert ist das Schloss Sanssouci. König Friedrich der Große hat es gebaut.

In English, some superlative adjectives add -*est*; in German, most add **-ste** and those with **a**, **o** and **u** add an umlaut. The ending agrees with the gender and case of the following noun: **das nördlichste Land**; **das größte Bundesland** (adjectives ending in s or ß omit the s in the ending).

G8

Auf Deutsch

2   Keith and Bella are on a **Kurzurlaub** *a short break/vacation* in the
     Nationalpark Unteres Odertal. Bella writes a postcard to her friend
     Hannelore. Read the postcard and use the glossary, if necessary. Then,
     decide whether the statements below are **richtig** *true* (**R**) or **falsch** *false* (**F**).

Liebe Hannelore,

wir sind seit zwei Tagen im Nationalpark. Uns gefällt der
Nationalpark, weil es hier viel zu sehen gibt. Wenn du gerne
aktiv bist, kann man hier viel machen. Es gibt viele kleine Dörfer
in der Nähe. Morgen mieten wir zwei Fahrräder und erkunden die
Gegend.

Heute Abend gibt es einen Vortrag über den Klimawandel und die
Konsequenzen für den Nationalpark. Das ist sehr interessant,
weil wir uns für die Natur interessieren.

Liebe Grüße
Bella

a   Keith und Bella mögen den Nationalpark.
b   Im Nationalpark gibt es nicht viel zu sehen.
c   Aktive Personen können hier viel machen.
d   In der Nähe gibt es keine Dörfer.
e   Keith und Bella machen morgen eine Fahrradtour.
f   Heute Abend gibt es einen Film über den globalen Klimawandel.

3   Using Bella's postcard as a model, write a card to your friend Heidemarie
     saying:

     – you have been in Bavaria for five days;
     – you like it because you can do a lot there;
     – there's a big castle nearby;
     – tomorrow you're hiring a car and exploring the villages;
     – this evening there is a wine festival. This is very interesting because
        you're interested in wine.

Dürfen *may, to be allowed to* and **mögen** *to like* are irregular
modal verbs, used like **können** and **müssen**.

ich	darf	mag	wir	dürfen	mögen
du	darfst	magst	ihr	dürft	mögt
er/sie/es/man	darf	mag	sie/Sie	dürfen	mögen

G15

Auf Deutsch

4   Friends of Keith and Bella, the Smith family, are spending a few days in a **Wellness-Zentrum** in Jena before they embark on their **Wanderurlaub.**

They have **einige Fragen** *a few questions* about their fitness programme and want to e-mail the manager, Herr Burgsmüller. Finish the e-mail Mr Smith has started.

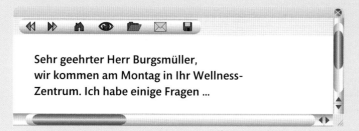

Sehr geehrter Herr Burgsmüller,
wir kommen am Montag in Ihr Wellness-
Zentrum. Ich habe einige Fragen ...

a   Kann man im Hotel schwimmen?

b   Must I train every day?

c   May we watch TV?

d   Can we explore the area?

e   Must we get up early?

f   May one relax in the evening?

5   Mrs Smith is making last minute preparations for the **Wanderurlaub**. Eager to use her German, she has written out a list of things she needs. Fill the gaps with the appropriate endings – some gaps may not need to be filled.

Ich brauche ...

ein<u>en</u> gelb<u>en</u> Rucksack (m)

a   ein... groß... Taschenlampe (f)

b   ein... klein... Handtuch *towel* (n)

c   ein... braun... Hut (m)

d   ein... rot... Jacke (f)

e   ein... schön... Sonnenbrille (f)

f   ein... dunkelblau... Hose (f)

g   ein... gut... Fernglas (n) *binoculars*

There are a few rules for the formation of plurals, but also many exceptions, so it is best to learn a new noun with its gender <u>and</u> its plural form (the nominative plural form given in the dictionary is the same as the accusative and genitive plural, but the dative plural adds an **-n** if there isn't one there already).

In general, many masculine nouns form their plural with **-e** plus an umlaut on **a**, **o** or **u**, feminine nouns with **-(e)n** and neuter nouns with **-er** plus an umlaut on **a**, **o** or **u**.

The definite article in the plural is **die**, regardless of gender.

6   Mrs Smith decides to use the same list to organise her whole family's packing. Supply the correct plural forms in the gaps.

	1 Rucksack	4 Rucksäcke
a	1 Taschenlampe	4 …
b	1 Handtuch	4 …
c	1 Hut	4 …
d	1 Jacke	4 …
e	1 Sonnenbrille	4 …
f	1 Hose	4 …
g	1 Fernglas *binoculars*	4 …

Was für ein schönes Haus!

reading property descriptions

describing a property

enquiring about renting a villa

showing someone round a house

In Deutschland ...

large numbers of visitors prefer to rent a **Ferienwohnung** *holiday flat* or a **Ferienhaus** *holiday home* than stay in a hotel. And there's always the alternative to buy a **Ferienimmobilie** *holiday property* – either by the **Nordsee** *North Sea* or **Ostsee** *Baltic Sea* in **Norddeutschland**. Or, if you prefer **Süddeutschland**, you may be able to find a **Landhaus** *country house* in **Bayern**, complete with **Panoramablick** *panoramic view* of the **Berge** *mountains*. Or how about **Österreich** or **die Schweiz**?

Natur, Kultur und Vielfalt *variety* are the great attractions that Germany and other German-speaking countries can offer.

Reading property descriptions

VERKAUF

Neugebautes Einfamilienhaus mit Blick aufs Meer:
Einfamilienhaus, Neubau, 2 Etagen, 3 Schlafzimmer,
2 Badezimmer, 1 Toilette, große Garage und Garten.
In hügeliger Lage, ca. 2 km von fantastischem Strand, in
Panorama-Lage mit Blick aufs Meer **Preis: €600.000**

EINMALIGE GELEGENHEIT: Altbau-Wohnung zu verkaufen in
wunderschönem Mietshaus, komplett renoviert, in historischem
Stadtkern. Diele, Wohnzimmer, drei Schlafzimmer, Badezimmer,
Wohnküche, Abstellraum, Terrasse. Preis: Verhandlungsbasis

REIHENHAUSWOHNUNG, Neubau, zentral gelegen.
Preis: €280.000.

WIR VERKAUFEN: PERFEKT RENOVIERTES LANDHAUS,
günstig gelegen, mit schöner Aussicht, 2 Kilometer vom
Stadtzentrum, Diele, Wohnzimmer, Esszimmer, Küche, vier
Schlafzimmer, 2 Badezimmer, Keller von 50 qm Größe, Garage
und Garten. Sonnige Lage, ruhig, aber nicht abgelegen.
Preis: €840.000

---

1 Look at the property profiles from the **Immobilienmakler** *estate agent*
and see how many of the words you know or can guess. Then work
through the profiles systematically, consulting the glossary where you
need to, and list:

a 5 types of dwellings **b** 9 different rooms
c 3 outside features **d** 6 adjectives describing location

Describing a property

1 1•56 Listen to the key language:

Können Sie (mir) ... beschreiben?	Can you describe ... (to me)?
Ihr Haus/Ihre Wohnung	your house/your flat
dein Haus oder deine Wohnung	your house or your flat (**du**)
Wie ist euer Haus?	What's your house like (**ihr**)?
meine/unsere Wohnung	my/our flat
Es/sie befindet sich ...	It's (located) ...

2 1•57 Listen as a) a woman living on her own, b) a couple and c) a young man living with friends are asked about where they live, and jot down *a*, *b* or *c* by the words in the boxes that describe their houses. You won't hear all these words.

Einfamilienhaus	**praktisch**	**günstig gelegen**
Landhaus	**renovierungsbedürftig**	**in ruhiger Lage**
Neubau-Wohnung	**alt**	**Panoramablick**
Reihenhaus	**zentral gelegen**	**modern**
Bauernhof	**gemütlich**	**renoviert**

Auf Deutsch

Possessive adjectives change their ending to agree in gender, case and number with the following noun, e.g. **mein Bauernhof** (m nom.), **meine Wohnung** (f nom.), **mein Haus** (n nom. + acc.). They follow the same pattern as the indefinite article **ein**.

my	*your* (du)	*his, its*	*her, its*	*our*	*your* (ihr)	*their*	*your* (Sie)
mein	dein	sein	ihr	unser	euer	ihr	Ihr

G9

---

3 1•58 The couple go on to describe their house in detail. Listen and decide:

- how many bedrooms it has;
- how many bathrooms;
- whether it has a garage;
- what's special about the terrace.

Enquiring about renting a villa

1 Anna Kiel from the UK has found this advert for a **Ferienhaus** in Husum, which is **zu vermieten** *for rent.*

Das Ferienhaus Strandparadies befindet sich 10 Minuten vom Meer und ist in der Nähe der Geschäfte. Guter Ausgangspunkt für Ausflüge an die Küste und den Hafen. Kann 6 bis 9 Personen beherbergen.
- **Erdgeschoss**: geräumiges Wohnzimmer mit Kamin und Doppelschlafcouch, ausgestattete Küche, Badezimmer, Dusche
- **zweite Etage**: Elternschlafzimmer (+ 1 Einzelbett), 2 Schlafzimmer (1 mit Etagenbett), Badezimmer
- **Außengelände**, mit Stellplatz, Garten und Terrasse mit Panoramablick

Mietpreis: Jan-März €775/Apr-Jun €875/Jul-Aug €1250/Sept-Okt €875

How would Anna tell her English partner:
a how many bedrooms and bathrooms the villa has?
b how far it is from the sea?
c whether there's anywhere to park the car?
d what there is to do locally?
e how much it will cost for a week in August?

2 1●59 Listen to the key language:

Können Sie mir ... geben?	Can you give me ...?
Ich beabsichtige ... zu ...	I intend to ...
... (zu) mieten	... to rent
Wie viele ...?	How many ...?

If there are two verbs in a clause, the infinitive at the end is usually preceded by zu, unless the first verb is a modal (e.g. **können**):
Er beabsichtigt, Deutsch zu lernen.
Ich hoffe *hope*, heute Abend ins Restaurant zu gehen.

3 1●60 Anna rings another **Ferienhaus**. Listen to her conversation with the owner and jot down the information she's given.

a Wie viele Schlafzimmer gibt es? **d** Gibt es eine Spülmaschine?
b Gibt es einen Garten? **e** Ist es in der Nähe vom Meer?
c Kann man parken? **f** Was kostet es pro Woche?

Showing someone round a house

1 **1•61** Listen to the key language:

Wie schön!	How lovely!
Was für ein schönes Zimmer!	What a beautiful room!
Es ist sehr/ein bisschen …	It's very/a bit …
Es ist ziemlich/so …	It's rather/so …
Vergessen Sie nicht, dass …	Don't forget that …
Machen Sie es sich gemütlich.	Make yourselves at home.

2 **1•62** Anna and her family decide to rent the **Strandparadies**. Listen as they're shown round, then fit **sehr**, **ein bisschen**, **so** and **ziemlich** into the gaps.

- ● Also, hier ist das Wohnzimmer.
- ◆ Was für ein schönes Zimmer! Und …. groß und was für eine Aussicht!
- ● Hier haben wir die Küche – sie ist …. geräumig *spacious*. Der Ofen, die Spülmaschine und der Kühlschrank sind neu.
- ◆ Gibt es keine Waschmaschine?
- ● Ja, doch, aber sie ist im Keller. Hier sind die Gästeschlafzimmer. Das Schlafzimmer rechts hat ein Doppelbett, und das Schlafzimmer links hat ein Etagenbett.
- ◆ Es ist …. klein.
- ● Es ist …… kompakt, das stimmt. Hier haben wir das Elternschlafzimmer. Und vergessen Sie nicht, dass das Wohnzimmer eine Schlafcouch hat. Also, machen Sie es sich gemütlich! Guten Aufenthalt! *Enjoy your stay!*

> When you join two sentences using **dass** *that*, the word order is the same as with **wenn** and **weil** clauses: **Vergessen Sie nicht, dass das Wohnzimmer eine Schlafcouch hat.**
>
> **G21**

Auf Deutsch

3 **1•63** Listening out for the key words **hundert** *100* and **tausend** *1000*, write down how much these properties cost:

a	Zweifamilienhaus *two-family house* mit Garage	………
b	herrliche Neubau-Wohnung	………
c	perfekt renoviertes Landhaus	………
d	Einfamilienhaus, fünf Zimmer	………
e	Landhaus mit fantastischer Aussicht	………

put it all together

1   From this list of words, find six pairs of opposites, e.g. **groß**
    and **klein**. You're left with one word – which is it and what
    does it mean in English?

Küste	Keller	zentral	kompakt	groß
abgelegen	Berge	klein	Land	
geräumig	Stadt	alt	neu	

2   What's the German for the labelled areas?

3   Write in German a profile of these two properties, of the kind
    used to advertise places for sale or rent.

a
> **Zu vermieten** Villa, new-build, with sea view, 5 mins
> from the sea. Garden + sunny terrace. 3 beds, 2 baths.

b
> **Zu verkaufen** Spacious country house with panoramic
> view, quiet but not isolated. Ground floor: entrance
> hall, living room, fitted kitchen, utility room. 1st floor:
> 4 bedrooms, bathroom. Large garden + garage.

Now write a similar short description of your home.

now you're talking!

1 **1•64** You call the Haus Ostsee for information. At the end, you need **Auf Wiederhören**, not **Auf Wiedersehen** as in a face-to-face situation.

- **Haus Ostsee, guten Morgen.**
- ◆ Say you're intending to rent a house in North Germany. Ask if he'll describe the Haus Ostsee for you.
- **Es ist ein schönes Reihenhaus mit Garten und Terrasse.**
- ◆ Ask if it's near the sea.
- **Es befindet sich drei oder vier Kilometer von einem herrlichen Strand.**
- ◆ Ask how much it costs per week.
- **€1500.**
- ◆ It's not cheap. Ask how many bedrooms the house has.
- **Das Haus hat drei Schlafzimmer. Es ist aber möglich, bis zu neun Personen zu beherbergen.**
- ◆ And how many bathrooms are there?
- **Es gibt ein großes Badezimmer auf der ersten Etage.**
- ◆ Hmm, a bit short on facilities. Ask if there's a washing machine.
- **Ja, aber sicher.**
- ◆ Is there a dishwasher?
- **Nein, eine Spülmaschine gibt es nicht.**
- ◆ You've heard enough! Say *Well, thank you and goodbye.*

2 **1•65** You decided against the Haus Ostsee but found a house near Timmendorf. Someone you meet asks you about it.

- **Wie ist Ihr Haus?**
- ◆ Say it's a country house.
- **Wo befindet es sich?**
- ◆ Say it's 10 km from Timmendorf.
- **Ist es ein großes Haus? Wie viele Zimmer hat das Haus?**
- ◆ Say the house has six rooms.
- **Sechs! Und wie viele Badezimmer?**
- ◆ Say there are three bathrooms.
- **Prima! Haben Sie einen Garten?**
- ◆ Say there's a small garden and a beautiful terrace.
- **Also – auf Wiedersehen und guten Aufenthalt.**

quiz

1 What sort of building is a **Mietshaus**?

2 If a property is **renovierungsbedürftig**, what state is it in?

3 What are the two words that tell you that there's somewhere to park your car?

4 What goes into a **Spülmaschine**?

5 When talking to a couple you've just met about their **Einfamilienhaus**, do you use **dein**, **euer** or **Ihr**?

6 If **Was für ein schönes Haus** means *What a beautiful house*, how would you say *What a beautiful room*?

7 To say *It's rather expensive* what word do you need in the gap? **Es ist .... teuer.**

8 Which is the odd one out: **hügelig**, **gemütlich**, **komfortabel**?

Now check whether you can ...

- understand the key words in property descriptions
- make enquiries about renting a holiday property
- describe your own home
- show someone round your house
- comment and pay a compliment on a house
- understand prices in hundreds and thousands of euros

Memory-training techniques can be used to good effect when learning a language. Start with a simple sentence such as **Ich möchte ein Haus in Deutschland** then add to it in small increments: **Ich möchte ein Haus in Deutschland mit Terrasse**, adding more as you mentally zoom in: **Ich möchte ein Haus in Deutschland mit Terrasse und einer großen Küche ... und drei Badezimmern ... und einem Keller** – until you're describing your ideal property in detail and creating a substantial sentence in German.

Ich habe meinen Laptop verloren

asking the way

... and following directions

explaining what's happened

reporting a problem

In Germany ...

if you lose your **Laptop**, **Portemonnaie** *purse*, **Brieftasche** *wallet*
or **Handy** *mobile*, you'll need to report the incident (**eine
Anzeige machen**).

Unless it constitutes an emergency – in which case you ring 110 – your first
port of call will be the nearest **Polizeirevier** *police station*. You could also
try the **Fundbüro** *lost-property office*.

Asking the way

1   2•01 Listen to the key language:

Können Sie mir/uns helfen?	Can you help me/us?
Wo befindet sich ...?	Where's ... (located)?
Sind Sie zu Fuß?	Are you on foot?
Haben Sie verstanden?	Have you understood?

2   2•02 Leo Brand and his wife Sigrid are looking for the **Polizeirevier** to report a lost **Laptop**. The rambling directions given by a passer-by include some of the following phrases. After you've familiarised yourself with these, listen and tick them off as you hear them.

die Straße runter *down the street*		**auf der linken Seite** *on your left*
bis zur Ampel *as far as the lights*		**Sie müssen ... nehmen.** *You have to take ...*
Gehen Sie rechts/links. *Go/Turn right/left.*		**Gehen Sie die Straße entlang.** *Follow/Go along the road.*
Gehen Sie in die ... Straße. *Turn into ... street.*		**Überqueren Sie ...** *Cross ...*
Gehen Sie immer geradeaus. *Go/Carry straight on.*		**dort am Ende** *there at the end*
in Richtung Bahnhof *towards the station*		

Instructions and directions use the **Sie** form of the verb + **Sie**:

Entschuldigen Sie (mich)! *Excuse me.*
Gehen Sie geradeaus! *Go straight on.*
Überqueren Sie den Platz! *Cross the square.*

G20

Auf Deutsch

3   2•03 In reply to **Haben Sie verstanden?** Leo had a go at recapping the directions given from notes he'd made. Listen and compare his summary to the original directions. What difference can you find?

... and following directions

4 **1•04** Leo needs to **Geld abheben** *withdraw some cash* on the way and asks a passer-by for the nearest cashpoint **Wo gibt es hier in der Nähe einen Geldautomaten?** Make a note of the directions you hear. Where exactly is the **Geldautomat** located?

5 **1•05** Listen to the key language:

Geht diese Straße zu ...?	Is this the way to ...?
Sie sind auf der falschen Straße.	You're in the wrong street.
Die Haltestelle ist ganz in der Nähe.	The (bus) stop is nearby.
Sie müssen ... aussteigen.	You have to get off ...

Some prepositions are followed by the accusative, e.g. **für** *for*, **bis** *as far as*, **entlang** *along* (which is unusual in going after the noun). Others are followed by the dative, e.g. **bei** *by*, **zu** *to*, **von** *from*.

An *on, at*; **auf** *on (top of)*, *in*; **vor** *in front of, before*; and **hinter** *behind* are followed by the dative when describing location, and the accusative when describing destination.

Das ist in der Bahnhofstraße. *It's in Bahnhofstraße.* (location)

Gehen Sie in die Rathausstraße. *Go to Rathausstraße.* (destination)

Zu combines with **der** (dat. f) and **dem** (dat. m, n) to give **zur** and **zum**: **zur Bank**; **zum Rathaus**. Similarly, **an** becomes **am** and **in** becomes **im** (note that there's no special feminine form as with **zu**).

G14

Auf Deutsch

6 **1•06** Sigrid asks someone else if they're going the right way to the **Polizeirevier**. Listen then see if you could interpret the reply.

a The police station is ....

b They can catch the number .... bus.

c The bus stop is ....

d They need to get off at ....

e The road they need is ....

f The police station is located ....

Explaining what's happened

1   **2•07** Listen to the key language:

Ich habe .... verloren.	I (have) lost ...
Ich habe gesagt ...	I (have) said ...
Was hast du gemacht?	What did you do?
Hast du eine Anzeige gemacht?	Have you reported it?
noch nicht	not yet
Er/sie hat angerufen.	He/she (has) phoned.

2   **2•08** Leo rings their friend Stefanie with a problem. Listen and then fit these verbs in the right place.

machen	habe	verloren	gemacht	hat
hast	gesagt	habe	verloren	habe

- ● Hallo Stefanie. Hier ist Leo
- ◆ Hallo, Leo, wie geht's?
- ● Hör mal, Stefanie, ich ...... meinen Laptop ....
- ◆ Wie? Was ..... du .....?
- ● Ich ....: Ich ..... meinen Laptop .....!
- ◆ Hast du eine Anzeige gemacht?
- ● Nein, noch nicht. Aber das ..... ich sofort.
- ◆ Gut, dann viel Glück! Bis bald *See you soon*!

Auf Deutsch

To talk about the past, i.e. *I (have) said; Did you see/Have you seen?*, you use the present tense of **haben** + the past participle of the main verb, which goes at the end of the sentence. For the past participle of regular/weak verbs, remove the **-en** of the infinitive, replace it with **-t**, and add **ge-** to the beginning of the word: **machen → gemacht**. Verbs with inseparable prefixes such as **ver-, be-, ent-, er-** don't need the **ge-**: **verstehen → verstanden**. In separable verbs, the **ge-** goes between the prefix and the base verb: **anrufen → angerufen**.

The past participle of irregular/strong verbs ends in **-en** and these have to be learnt individually: **sehen → gesehen**; **essen → gegessen**; **verlieren → veloren**.

G20

3   **2•09** Leo then rings Frank to say *We're running late* (**Wir verspäten uns**). Can you work out why Sigrid's irritated?

Reporting a problem

1 2•10 Listen to the key language:

Was kann ich für Sie tun?	What can I do for you?
jemand/niemand	someone/no one
Haben Sie etwas/jemanden gesehen?	Did you see anything/ anyone?
Ich habe nichts/niemanden gesehen.	I saw nothing/no one.

2 After taking Leo's details, the **Polizist** *police officer* takes a statement of what happened. Before you listen, work out the infinitives of these past participles and check their meaning in the glossary: **gesucht, gesteckt, gestellt**.

3 2•11 Listen to Leo's statement and then arrange these events in the order they happened, starting with **Ich habe Briefmarken gekauft**.

  a Ich habe bezahlt.
  b Ich habe ihn nicht gesehen.
  c Ich habe den Laptop gesucht.
  d Ich habe den Laptop auf den Boden gestellt.
  e Ich habe die Brieftasche und die Brille in die Tasche gesteckt.

4 Imagine you were at the post office and describe what Leo did.

> **Jemand** *someone* and **niemand** *no one* become **jemanden** and **niemanden** in the accusative (i.e. when they become the direct object of the sentence): **Ich habe niemanden gesehen**. *I didn't see anyone/I saw nobody/I haven't seen anyone.*

Auf Deutsch

5 Choose the correct word from the brackets.

  a .... hat verstanden. (niemand/niemanden)
  b Haben Sie .... in der Nähe gesehen? (jemand/ jemanden)
  c .... hat einen Laptop verloren. (jemand/jemanden)

put it all together

1 Which one would you use:

Ich habe das Polizeirevier angerufen.

Was haben Sie gemacht?

Was hast du gesagt?

Ich habe nicht verstanden.

Ich habe nichts gesehen.

Ich habe niemanden gesehen.

a to ask somebody what s/he said;
b to say you've seen nobody;
c to say you've seen nothing;
d to say you've called the police station;
e to say you haven't understood;
f to ask a group of people what they've done?

2 Make past participles from the verbs in the box and then use them to fill in the blanks below.

a Ich habe meinen Pass ......
b Habt ihr das Haus ......?
c Wir haben das Dokument ......
d Er hat ein Eis ......
e Leo hat seinen Laptop auf den Boden ......
f Hast du einen Stadtplan ......
g Ich habe meine Schuhe ......
h Er hat seine Sekretärin *secretary* ......

verstehen
verlieren
sehen
stellen
essen
anrufen
kaufen
suchen

3 Check your answers for Activity 2, then replace the object of each sentence (i.e. passport, document, etc.) with *it* (**ihn/sie/es**) or *them* (**sie**). These are the pronouns in the object, accusative, case. If you need to, go back to Unit 5 or check page 137.

The first is done for you:

a **Ich habe meinen Pass verloren. Ich habe ihn verloren.**

1 2•12 You're staying in Germany, and you and your partner need to get to the nearest police station.

- Stop a man in the street and ask if he can help you (both).
- ◆ **Ja, was kann ich für Sie tun?**
- Find out where the police station's located.
- ◆ **In der Weststraße.**
- You set off, thinking you knew where Weststraße was, but now you're lost. Stop a woman and ask if this road goes to the police station.
- ◆ **Ja, es ist nicht weit. Gehen Sie die Straße runter bis zur Ampel. Dort gehen Sie links. Gehen Sie dann die Straße entlang bis zur Marktstraße, dann rechts und Sie finden die Weststraße auf der linken Seite. Das Polizeirevier ist am Ende der Straße, auf der rechten Seite. Haben Sie verstanden?**
- Tell her, yes, you've understood and thank her.

2 Now translate for your partner the directions to the **Polizeirevier** in Weststraße.

3 2•13 Paul Hölzner, a colleague, has left you a message saying there's an urgent problem, so you ring him. Use **du**.

- **Paul Hölzner.**
- ◆ Greet Paul and ask him if there is a problem.
- **Ja, Stefan hat …**
- ◆ You didn't catch that so ask what he said.
- **Stefan hat sein Handy verloren. Hast du es gesehen?**
- ◆ Say you saw it yesterday (**gestern**) at Frauke's house (**bei Frauke**).
- **Er hat alles verloren – Daten, Termine, Telefonnummern. Er ist total gestresst.**
- ◆ Ask if he has phoned Frauke.
- **Nein, noch nicht … Und ihr zwei, was habt ihr heute gemacht?**
- ◆ Say you went on a trip (**einen Ausflug machen**) to Cologne.
- **Und wo habt ihr gegessen?**
- ◆ You ate lunch at a **Kneipe** (f) on the **Rathausplatz**.
- **Prima!**

quiz

1 What's the emergency phone number in Germany and what's the German for *police station*?

2 How far is **ganz in der Nähe**?

3 If somebody says to you **Haben Sie verstanden?**, what do they want to know?

4 Does **etwas** or **jemand** mean *something*?

5 If **falsche Straße** means *wrong street*, how would you say *wrong number*?

6 How would you ask if you're going the right way to the station?

7 On a bus, to ask where you have to get off is **Wo muss ich ....?**

8 If **kaufen** is *to buy* and **verkaufen** is *to sell*, how do you say *I bought* and *I sold*?

Now check whether you can ...

- ask the way to a particular place
- follow directions to get there
- say if you've understood or not
- talk about having to do something
- say what you've done
- explain what others have done

You're more than halfway through *Talk German 2* – a good time to bring together some of the vocabulary from the six units you've covered. For example:

- Say what time you ate yesterday using the perfect tense of **zu Mittag essen** *to have lunch* and **zu Abend essen** *to have dinner/supper*.
- Using **Heute habe ich ... gesehen**, list as many things you've seen today as you can. Or as many members of your family (if you haven't seen any of them, say you've seen nobody today).

Noch mehr! 3

1   Paul and Sarah May are planning to rent a holiday home in Switzerland and have listed their requirements. Read about these two places and put a ✓ or ✗ against them to show whether they fit the bill. If no information is available, put a ?.

		1	2
●	within reach of **Blausee Naturpark**		
●	quiet location		
●	shops not too far		
●	somewhere to eat outside		
●	car parking		
●	sleeps four comfortably		
●	two bathrooms		
●	large kitchen		
●	heating (it can be cold in the mountains)		

1

ZU VERMIETEN Einfamilienhaus, Neubau, in einem kleinen, ruhigen Bergdorf, in der Nähe vom Naturpark Blausee, mitten im Berner Oberland.
Vier bis fünf Betten, Unterkunft umfasst eine kleine Diele, Wohnzimmer, geräumige Bauernküche, Badezimmer, separate Toilette, zwei Schlafzimmer (mit Einbauschränken). Blick auf die Berge, mit kleiner Terrasse. Stellplatz auf Anfrage.

2

ZU VERMIETEN Berghaus Kandersteg, Berghütte, komplett renoviert, in ruhiger Lage. Fünf km von Blausee entfernt.
Mit herrlichem Panorama auf das Tal. Die Unterkunft hat ein geräumiges Wohnzimmer mit großem Kamin; eine Eck-Kochnische, sechs Schlafplätze, zwei Badezimmer. Lebensmittelgeschäft, Bäckerei + Sportzentrum mit Schwimmbad ca. zwei km entfernt; Bushaltestelle 200 m. Garage möglich.

2 The Mays like the look of **Berghaus Kandersteg** and write to the **Besitzer** *owner*, asking for more information. See if you can read the letter without using the glossary, then check the English translation on page 119. Note the polite **Können Sie mir mitteilen/sagen ...?** *Can you tell me ...?* and **Wir möchten gerne erfahren ...** *We would like to know ...*

Herrn   18. Juli 2011
Wilhelm Waldbach
Bergstraße 5
3718 Kandersteg

Sehr geehrter Herr Waldbach,

ich beabsichtige, zwei Wochen mit meiner Frau und zwei
Freunden in der Nähe von Kandersteg und Blausee zu
verbringen. Können Sie mir bitte mitteilen, ob Ihr Haus, das
Berghaus Kandersteg, vom 22. September bis 6. Oktober frei
ist? Können Sie mir auch sagen, wie hoch die Wochenrate
für diese Zeitspanne ist, inklusive Gebrauchs der Garage?

Wir möchten auch gerne erfahren, ob es eine
Waschmaschine gibt und ob die Kochnische einen
Gefrierschrank hat.

Mit freundlichen Grüßen

P May

---

3 Imagine you and three friends are planning a week in Kandersteg and Blausee. Write a letter to Herr Waldbach, asking:

- if the **Berghaus Kandersteg** is free from 28th July to 4th August;
- the price including **Versicherung** (f) *insurance*;
- how many bedrooms there are and if there's a dishwasher.

4 While Sarah is **in der Schweiz** her friend Hannelore is on holiday in England. Sarah writes to her from Switzerland, saying **Es hat gut geschmeckt!** What was it that tasted good?

Read through the text to get an overall impression, then use the glossary, if necessary, to help you with the next two activities.

Liebe Hannelore,

gestern Morgen haben wir eine lange Wanderung im Naturpark gemacht. Wenn wir in den Bergen sind, gehen wir immer lange wandern! Wir haben sehr viel gesehen, haben den See besucht, und haben alles mit unserer neuen Kamera fotografiert. Am Nachmittag haben wir uns ein bisschen entspannt und haben im Hotel ferngesehen.

Als wir im Dorf waren, haben wir ein traditionelles Restaurant gefunden, wo wir am Abend gegessen haben. Wir haben ein Käsefondue probiert. Es hat sehr gut geschmeckt! Morgen muss ich viel trainieren, weil ein Käsefondue so viele Kalorien hat!

Was hast du gestern gemacht? Hast du schon das englische Essen probiert?

Hast du etwas gekauft? Wann bist du wieder in Deutschland?

Schreibe mir bald!

Sarah

5 Make a list of all the past participles (list each only once) and write down their infinitives, e.g: **gemacht – machen**. (The past participle of verbs ending in **-ieren**, e.g. **probieren**, **fotografieren**, replaces **-ieren** with **-t**. There's no **ge-: probiert**.)

6 Writing as Hannelore, tell Sarah about your stay in England.

- Begin your message with an appropriate greeting.
- Say that yesterday afternoon you visited the museum and the castle. In the village you bought **ein Buch** *a book*.
- Say that you saw a lot and took many photos.
- Explain to Sarah that in the evening you tried *steak and kidney pie* – it didn't taste very good!
- Ask her to write to you soon.

The English *when* is translated in various ways in German.

When meaning *whenever* or describing a regular event is **wenn**: **Wenn wir in den Bergen sind, wandern wir jeden Tag.** *When(ever) we're in the mountains we walk every day.*

Wenn also means *if*.

When in the past tense is **als**: **Als wir in der Schweiz waren, haben wir Bern besucht.** *When we were in Switzerland, we visited Bern.* Like **wenn**, **als** sends the verb to the end.

When as a question word (direct or indirect) is **wann**: **Wann beginnt das Konzert? Können Sie mir sagen, wann das Konzert beginnt?**

7 Read the statement Rüdiger Welling made after losing his wallet, then find the 11 errors in the official **Verlustanzeige** *loss report*.

Ich heiße Rüdiger Welling. Ich wohne in Würzburg, in der Mayerhoferstraße 23. Ich bin 33 Jahre alt. Ich bin 1979 in Ratingen geboren.

Gestern Nachmittag, am Montag, den 5. März, im Sportzentrum in der Goethestraße, habe ich meinem Freund, Oliver, ein schönes Foto von meiner Verlobten Dagmar, gezeigt. Dann habe ich meine Brieftasche (mit dem Foto, 200 Euro, Führerschein) in meinen Rucksack gesteckt. Die Brieftasche ist aus schwarzem Leder und hat fünfunddreißig Euro gekostet.

Dagmar hat mich angerufen, und ich habe meinen Rucksack auf den Boden gestellt. Nach ein paar Minuten habe ich das Sportzentrum mit meinem Rucksack verlassen. Als ich meinen Rucksack zu Hause geöffnet habe, war meine Brieftasche nicht da.

Der Unterzeichnende: Name, Vorname | Wahrig, Rüdiger

geboren in | 93047 Regensburg | am | 4. November 1979

wohnhaft in | Hofstraße 26, 97070 Würzburg

Telefonnummer (mit Vorwahl) | 0931-8274827

Pass ☑ oder Ausweis ☐ Nummer: | 1458397145

gültig bis | 24. Oktober 2015 | erklärt

den/die folgenden Artikel | Brieftasche aus braunem Leder

Inhalt = €300, Pass, 1 Foto, Gesamtwert €350

☑ als verloren

Verlustdatum (Tag, Datum) | Dienstag, 6. März | um (Uhrzeit) | 10.00

Verlustort | Einkaufszentrum

Verlustereignis | Brieftasche in Jackentasche gelassen

---

zeigen *to show* **der Führerschein** *driving licence* **verlassen** *to leave* **öffnen** *to open* **wohnhaft in** *resident in* **erklären** *to declare, explain* **der Ort** *location* **das Ereignis** *event*

Warst du schon einmal auf Rügen?

talking about holiday plans

saying what the weather's like

talking about previous holidays

... and describing what happened

In Deutschland ...

the varied landscape of **Meer**, **Land**, **Großstadt** *big city* and **Berge** makes it an attractive destination for both German and foreign tourists. While many Germans prefer holidaying abroad, many stay in the country and head for the **Strand** *beach* or a **Bergsee** *mountain lake*, or perhaps venture **in die Schweiz** or **Österreich** to enjoy the increasingly popular **Aktivurlaub** or **Wellnessurlaub**. A winter favourite is **der Wintersporturlaub** *winter sports holiday*.

If you're planning an outdoor activity, you'll need to understand **die Wettervorhersage** *weather forecast* or **Wetterbericht** *weather report*. You might be interested in the **Freizeitwetter** *leisure weather forecast*, **Wintersportwetter** or even **Biowetter** – a weather forecast based on the notion that weather is responsible for certain illnesses!

Talking about holiday plans

1   2•14 Listen to the key language:

Wohin fahren Sie/fährst du ...	Where are you going ...
dieses Jahr/diesen Sommer?	... this year/this summer?
... auf Urlaub?	... on holiday?
Ich fahre/Wir fahren ...	I'm going/We're going ...
Ich hoffe, ... zu fahren.	I hope to go ...
Ihr Glücklichen!	Lucky you (pl)!

2   2•15 As part of an **Umfrage** *survey*, people are asked where they're going on holiday this year. Read these replies given by those holidaying in a German-speaking country, then listen and tick the five you hear.

- ☐ Ich fahre mit meiner Freundin ans Meer.
- ☐ Auf die Insel Rügen, mit meiner Familie. Ich habe die Insel noch nie *never before* gesehen.
- ☐ Ich hoffe, nach Regensburg zu fahren.
- ☐ Wir fahren in die Berge nach Mariazell.
- ☐ Dieses Jahr bleibe ich zu Hause.
- ☐ Diesen Sommer fahre ich zu meiner Tante. Sie wohnt in der Nähe von Bern.
- ☐ Ich fahre mit meinen Freunden nach München.
- ☐ Wir fahren in den Schwarzwald. Mein Bruder hat ein Landhaus fünfzehn Kilometer von Freiburg.

> **Auf Deutsch**
>
> The English to *go* can be **gehen**, implying going on foot, or **fahren** when there's transport involved. **Fahren** is irregular in the **du** and **er/sie/es** forms only: **du fährst, er/sie/es fährt**.

3   2•16 Here's the reply from another person who took part in the **Umfrage** and who's heading off **alleine** *on her own*. Work out which form of **fahren** goes in the gaps; then listen and check your answers.

- ● Entschuldigen Sie bitte, wohin .... Sie dieses Jahr auf Urlaub?
- ◆ Diesen Sommer hoffe ich nach Lübeck zu .... – alleine! Ich bin geschieden und meine Tochter .... mit meinem Ex-Mann auf Urlaub. Sie .... in die Karibik – zur Oma.

Saying what the weather's like

Es ist sonnig.

Es ist wechselhaft.

Es ist bewölkt.

Es ist nebelig.

Es regnet.

Es ist windig

Es schneit.

Es ist schrecklich!
It's awful!

Es gibt Schauer.

Es gibt Gewitter.

Es ist warm.

Es ist kalt.

Es ist heiß.

To talk about the weather in the present, you say:
Es ist heiß/windig.
Es gibt Schauer/Gewitter.
Es regnet/schneit.

The equivalents, when talking about the past, are:
Es war heiß/windig. (imperfect)
Es gab Schauer/Gewitter. (imperfect)
Es hat geregnet/geschneit. (perfect)

G20

Auf Deutsch

---

1 **2•17** Siegfried, who's going to Bad Mergentheim, talks about the weather there. Listen, then make a note under these two headings of what he says about it. See if you can catch what the average temperature is in July and August. *Degrees* are **Grad**.

im Sommer *in summer*   **im Winter** *in winter*

....

....

Im Juli und August ist die Temperatur im Durchschnitt ..... Grad.

Talking about previous holidays

1   2•18 Listen to the key language:

Wohin bist du/seid ihr/ sind Sie ... gefahren?	Where did you go ...?
letztes Jahr	last year
Ich bin ... gefahren.	I went ...
Ich bin ... geblieben.	I stayed ...
Sie sind ... gekommen.	They came ...
Vor ... Jahren.	... years ago.

Some verbs form their perfect tense with **sein** + past participle, not with **haben**. Most of them relate to a change of place or state, e.g. **fahren, kommen, gehen, ankommen**, but **bleiben** *to stay* behaves in the same way: **ich bin gefahren** *I went*; **wir sind geblieben** *we stayed*; **sie sind angekommen** *they arrived*.   **G20**

2   2•19 In the same survey, people were asked where they went on holiday last year. Listen and number each statement in the order you hear it.

- Ich bin wie jedes Jahr in die Alpen gefahren. Ich gehe gern wandern.
- Ich bin zu meiner Oma nach England gefahren. Ich bin zwei Wochen geblieben.
- Letztes Jahr sind wir nicht auf Urlaub gefahren. Unsere Freunde aus Frankreich sind nach Deutschland gekommen.
- Ich bin nach Österreich gefahren, genauer gesagt nach Kufstein.
- Wir sind nach München gefahren. Es war sehr warm.
- Ich bin ans Meer gefahren.

3   In German, how would you say the following? The sequence is time, manner, place, past participle: **Er ist letztes Jahr** (time) **mit dem Schiff/ mit seiner Familie** (manner) **nach Griechenland** (place) **gefahren** (past participle).

a   *I went to Berlin with my girlfriend.*
b   *We went to the Caribbean last year by ship.*
c   *We went to England with friends.*
d   *Did you (***du***) go to Aachen yesterday?*

... and describing what happened

4 2•20 Listen to the key language:

Hattest du viel Spaß?	Did you have a lot of fun?
Es war ausgezeichnet!	It was superb.
Was habt ihr gemacht?	What did you do?
Warst du schon einmal auf Rügen?	Have you ever been to Rügen?
Ich war noch nie dort.	I have never been there.

5 2•21 Sebastian's back at work after a holiday. Listen as a colleague asks him about it and try to catch where he went and who he went with.

Wohin? ....   **Mit wem?** ....

6 2•21 Sebastian goes on to describe a memorable day on the island of Rügen, visiting the town of Putbus. Before you listen, read the jumbled-up version of events and number them in the order you predict the events occurred.

Gestiegen is the past participle of **steigen** *to climb*, while **zurückgekehrt** comes from **zurückkehren** *to return*. Both these verbs form the perfect tense with **sein**. **Zurückkehren** is a separable verb: **zurück-** means *back*.

a Wir haben fabelhaften Fisch gegessen.
b Wir sind mit der Fähre von Stralsund gefahren.
c Wir sind um sechs Uhr wieder in den Bus gestiegen.
d Wir sind mit dem Bus nach Putbus gefahren.
e Wir haben die Kirche im Schlosspark gesehen.
f Wir sind gegen elf Uhr in Altefähr angekommen.
g Wir sind ein bisschen durch die Straßen gegangen.
h Wir sind um neun Uhr abends nach Stralsund zurückgekehrt.
i Wir haben ein kleines Restaurant gefunden.
j Am Donnerstag sind wir nach Rügen gefahren.

put it all together

1   Match the picture with the description of the weather.

1   Es ist schrecklich!
2   Es ist heiß.
3   Es ist schön.
4   Es ist bewölkt.
5   Es ist kalt.
6   Es schneit.

2   Fill the gaps with the right form of **haben** or **sein** and the correct past participle.

a   ...... ihr schon ......? (essen)
b   ...... ihr mit dem Auto oder mit dem Zug ......? (fahren)
c   Ich ...... spät nach Hause ...... (kommen)
d   Stefan und Anna ...... auf den Berg ...... (steigen)
e   Renate ...... drei Wochen in Berlin ...... (bleiben)
f   ...... sie viel ......? (fotografieren)
g   Er ...... gestern ...... (zurückkehren)
h   Wann ...... Sie ......? (ankommen)
i   Wir ...... ein gutes Hotel ...... (finden)

3   Rewrite this passage as if you were Siegfried and it happened two years ago. The second sentence is made up of two clauses/verbs; treat each as a unit (the first past participle will go at the end of the clause, not the full sentence).

Dieses Jahr fahre ich mit meinen Freunden nach Rügen auf Urlaub. Wir fahren mit der Fähre von Stralsund und kommen in Altefähr an.

4   In reply to **Wohin fahren Sie auf Urlaub?** how would you say:
a   you're going to the sea by yourself;
b   you (and somebody else) are going to France with two friends;
c   you're going to Bavaria (**Bayern**) with your family;
d   you (and somebody else) aren't going on holiday this year; you're staying at home?

now you're talking!

1 **2•23** A German friend planning to come over to the UK rings you to ask what the weather's like.

- ● **Sag mal, wie ist das Wetter heute?**
- ◆ Tell him the weather's good, that it's sunny.
- ● **Ist es kalt?**
- ◆ Say no, it's 18°.

2 **2•24** Now talking about holidays – first, some questions about plans.

a
- ● **Wohin fährst du dieses Jahr auf Urlaub?**
- ◆ Say you're going to the seaside.
- ● **Fährst du alleine?**
- ◆ Say no, you're going with your friends.

b
- ● **Fahren Sie diesen Sommer nach Österreich?**
- ◆ Say yes, you're hoping to go to **Kärnten** with your partner (**Partner(in)**).
- ● **Eine schöne Region. Fahren Sie in die Berge?**
- ◆ Say yes and explain that your cousin (**Cousine**) has a house near Ratingen.
- ● **Sie Glücklichen! Ich war vor zwei Jahren dort.**

3 **2•25** And now some questions about last year's holiday.

- ● **Waren Sie schon einmal in Österreich?**
- ◆ Say you went to Austria last year. Add that you went with friends.
- ● **Hatten Sie viel Spaß?**
- ◆ Say it was superb.
- ● **Wie war das Wetter?**
- ◆ Say it was very hot, 35°.

4 How would you yourself reply to these questions?

- ● **Wohin fahren Sie dieses Jahr auf Urlaub?**
- ● **Wohin sind Sie letztes Jahr auf Urlaub gefahren?**

quiz

1 How would you say *three years ago*?

2 How would you say *I have never been to Germany*?

3 To ask a friend *Where are you going on holiday*? do you need **fahre, fährt, fahren** or **fährst**?

4 Can you think of one verb beginning with **k** and one verb beginning with **f** that use **sein** to form the past?

5 **Geblieben** is the past participle of which verb? What does it mean? Does it take **haben** or **sein** in the past?

6 How do you say in German that the weather's awful?

7 What's the difference between **es ist heiß** and **es war heiß**?

8 Which of these verbs doesn't form its past tense with **sein: gehen, anrufen, ankommen, steigen**?

Now check whether you can ...

- use **fahren** to say where you and other people are going
- talk about holiday plans: where you're going and who with
- say you're hoping to go somewhere
- talk about past holidays: say where you went and describe what you did
- comment on the weather

Now that you know how to talk about the past, you could either keep a simple diary in German or talk (to yourself or to anyone who'll listen and understand) about what you've been doing. Keep it simple and repetitive at first, using **Ich bin ... gefahren; Ich bin ... gekommen; Ich bin ... angekommen; Ich bin ... gegangen** and linking this with places. Then add detail, such as the time, what you saw, who you talked to and what the weather was like, using **das Wetter war ...**

Mir geht's nicht gut

saying how you're feeling

... and describing symptoms

following instructions

choosing alternative solutions

In Deutschland ...

Arzt and **Doktor** both mean *doctor*. You address him or her as
Herr/Frau Doktor.

EU citizens can make use of Germany's **Gesundheitswesen** *National Health
Service* provided they have a European Health Insurance Card (EHIC) but
will have to pay for services. If you ring any doctor outside surgery hours,
you will usually hear a pre-recorded message giving the telephone number
for the out-of-hours doctor (**Notarzt**). In an emergency, the number to dial
is 112 and the place to head for is the **Notaufnahme** *casualty department* of
the nearest **Krankenhaus** *hospital*.

Saying how you're feeling

1 **2•26** Listen to the key language:

Wie geht es Ihnen/dir?	How are you (**Sie/du**)?
Was ist los?	What's the matter with you?
Geht's dir nicht gut?	Aren't you feeling very well?
Mir/Ihm/Ihr geht's ...	I/He/She feel(s) ...
... gut, schlecht, furchtbar	... well, bad, dreadful
... gar nicht gut	... not at all well
Du Armer/Arme!	You poor thing (m/f)!
Gab es einen Unfall?	Has there been an accident?

2 Read this email from Sonja to Astrid. Why can't she meet up?

Von: Sonja Wichert   **Datum:** Montag, 1. Oktober 2012 06
An: Astrid Wagner   **Betreff:** mir geht's nicht gut

Hallo,
ich kann dich heute nicht zum Mittagessen treffen, weil ich
heute nicht zur Arbeit gehe. Mir geht's nicht gut. Tut mir leid.
Liebe Grüße
Sonja ☹

Auf Deutsch

To say how you feel, you use **Mir geht es/Mir geht's**. When
talking about how someone else feels, you replace **mir** with **dir**,
ihm, **ihr**, **uns**, **euch**, **ihnen** or **Ihnen**.   **G12**

3 **2•27** Listen as Astrid rings Sonja to find out what's wrong with her and
what happened on her trip **aufs Land** *to the country*, then fill the gaps.

- Ich ..... nicht laufen. Aua! Astrid, ... geht's so schlecht.
- Du Arme! Aber ..... ist los? Gab ..... einen Unfall?
- Einen Unfall? Nein. Gestern ..... ich mit Ludwig ausgegangen. Wir
  sind aufs Land ..... und ..... mindestens hundert Kilometer gewandert.
- Sonja, übertreibe nicht *don't exaggerate*!
- Na ja, mindestens ..... Kilometer. Und ich ..... gefallen.
- Sonja, ich habe ..... zu tun. Tschüs!

4 Write an email to Hans-Jörg, a mutual friend, explaining that Sonja's
not going into work today; she's not feeling well because she went to
the country with Ludwig yesterday and fell over.

... and describing symptoms

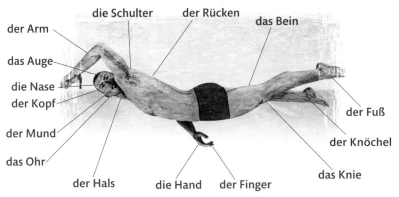

der Arm
die Schulter
der Rücken
das Bein
das Auge
die Nase
der Kopf
der Mund
das Ohr
der Hals
die Hand
der Finger
der Fuß
der Knöchel
das Knie

To say something's hurting, you can use:
- **Schmerzen haben: Ich habe Kopfschmerzen.** *I've got a headache.*
- **wehtun:**
  Mein Knie tut weh. *My knee hurts.*
  Meine Knie tun weh. *My knees hurt.*
  Tut deine/Tut Ihre Hand weh? *Does your hand hurt?*
  Sein/Ihr Knie tut weh. *His/her knee hurts.*

Auf Deutsch

5 **2•28** Astrid rings Sonja again later to ask if she's feeling any better **Geht's dir besser?** Listen and decide which parts of her are hurting.

6 **2•29** Sonja then rings her sister Gabriele whose response is to say **Ich kann heute nicht lange reden** *I can't chat* because her little boy Peter is ill. Read this list of potential symptoms, listen to Gabriele then tick off the ones Peter's displaying from the list.

   Sein Mund tut weh.
   Seine Nase tut weh.
   Sein Rücken tut weh.
   Seine Arme tun weh.
   Seine Schultern tun weh.
   Seine Augen tun weh.

   Er hat Ohrenschmerzen.
   Er hat Kopfschmerzen.
   Er hat Halsschmerzen.
   Er hat Magenschmerzen.
   Er hat Fieber.
   Er hat Husten *cough.*

Following instructions

1   **2•30** Listen to the key language:

Was ist passiert?	What's happened?
Ich habe .... verstaucht.	I've sprained ...
Nichts Ernstes.	Nothing serious.
Das Knie ist geprellt.	The knee is bruised.
Nehmen Sie ein Schmerzmittel.	Take a pain killer.
Ruhen Sie ...	Rest ...
... wird alles wieder in Ordnung sein.	... all will be back to normal.

2   **2•31** A couple of days later, Sonja hobbles to the doctor's. She finds it **schwierig** *difficult* to move her knee. Read this outline of their conversation with the aid of the glossary before you listen to it.

Her diagnosis:	**Ich habe mein Knie verstaucht.**
His diagnosis:	**Das Knie ist ein bisschen geprellt. Nichts Ernstes.**
His advice:	**Nehmen Sie ein Schmerzmittel, ruhen Sie und bewegen Sie es nicht viel.**
His prognosis:	**In zwei oder drei Tagen wird alles wieder in Ordnung sein.**

To talk about the future, you usually use the present tense with a time phrase or **werden** *will* + an infinitive, which goes at the end of the clause. **Werden** is irregular in the **du** (**wirst**) and **er/sie/es** forms (**wird**).

Ich nehme heute Abend ein Schmerzmittel. *I'll take a painkiller tonight.*

Ich werde ein Schmerzmittel nehmen. *I'll take a painkiller.*

3   **2•32** Sonja goes to the **Apotheke** *chemist* for some painkillers. Listen and see if you can pick out any of the **Apotheker**'s instructions, based on what you might expect to hear in English in the same circumstances. Then check the transcript on page 122.

You'll hear **überschreiten** *to exceed*, which has the same prefix as **übertreiben** *to exaggerate*.

Auf Deutsch

Choosing alternative solutions

HOLISTISCHE MEDIZIN
bringt die körperlichen, emotionalen, spirituellen und sozialen Dimensionen des Menschen in Harmonie

Moritz Beckmann – persönlicher Trainer
- Haben Sie genug vom Trainieren ohne Resultate?
- Haben Sie Ernährungsprobleme?

ICH STEHE IHNEN GERNE MIT MEINER LANGJÄHRIGEN ERFAHRUNG ZUR VERFÜGUNG.

AKKUPUNKTUR: ALTE MEDIZINISCHE PRAXIS AUS CHINA
kann Schmerzen, Arthritis, Hauterkrankungen, Menstruationsprobleme und Probleme in der Schwangerschaft behandeln.

SHIATSU
Online-Kurs zum Erlernen der japanischen Massagekunst

GESTRESST? ANGESPANNT?
HILFE FÜR DAS INNERE WOHLBEFINDEN: MEDITATION, ASTROLOGIE UND HOLISTISCHES COACHING

HOMÖOPATHIE

Kurse, Seminare und Informationen

Möchten Sie abnehmen?
Wählen Sie eine ausgewogene, persönliche Diät.
Kostenlose Beratung per E-Mail

---

1 Without the help of the glossary, have a look at these adverts taken from the notice board at the chemist's and see if you can find the German for: *acupuncture, balanced diet, harmony, holistic medicine, homeopathy, inner wellbeing, massage, personal trainer, stressed.*

put it **all together**

1   Find the odd one out in each line.

    a Knöchel, Auge, Ohr, Mund
    b Meditation, Trainer, Akkupunktur, Homöopathie
    c gestresst, angespannt, müde, gestern
    d Arm, Unfall, Schulter, Knie

2   Choose the correct ending for each sentence.

a Maria hat	**1** sehr schlecht.
b Ich kann es nicht	**2** einen Unfall.
c Es gab	**3** bewegen.
d Peter geht es	**4** Fieber.
e Ich bin	**5** gestern gewandert.

3   Write an e-mail in German to your friend Daniel, telling him:

- you're sorry but you can't meet him this evening;
- you're not well, you've got a temperature and your arms and legs hurt;
- Marion's got a sore throat and a headache.

Also, ask him how he is and whether:

- he went to work today;
- he's seen Uwe.

An: Daniel Rosslan
Datum: 1.11.2012
Betreff: heute Abend

1 **2•33** Imagine you're Ludwig, Sonja's boyfriend. It's the day after your walk in the country and you've rung her on her mobile.

- Say *Hi* and ask if she's well.
- ◆ **Nein, mir geht's nicht gut. Mir geht's gar nicht gut.**
- Ask what the matter is with her.
- ◆ **Mein Rücken tut weh und mein Knie tut weh.**
- She clearly needs sympathy. Say *You poor thing* and ask what happened.
- ◆ **Was ist passiert? Gestern ist passiert!**
- She's not making sense. Ask if she had fun yesterday.
- ◆ **Ludwig, gestern sind wir 20 Kilometer gewandert und heute kann ich nicht aufstehen. Ich kann nicht …**
- You need to stop the flow. Tell her the two of you walked five kilometres, then say you've got a lot to do.

2 **2•34** You're now going to describe a whole host of unpleasant symptoms of your own! You'll be asked if you have already taken something for them **Haben Sie etwas eingenommen?**

- ◆ **Wie geht es Ihnen heute?**
- Say you're not feeling well.
- ◆ **Das tut mir leid. Was ist los?**
- Say you've got a headache and a sore throat.
- ◆ **Sie Armer!**
- And your shoulders hurt.
- ◆ **Haben Sie Fieber?**
- Say yes, and you have a cough and earache.
- ◆ **Ich glaube, Sie haben Grippe. Haben Sie etwas eingenommen?**
- Say no but that you want a painkiller.
- ◆ **Ich habe ein sehr wirksames homöopathisches Medikament. Einen Augenblick, bitte …**

quiz

1 What's the German for the *casualty department* and what is the emergency phone number in Germany?

2 How would you say *She feels better*?

3 How would you say in German that a) your foot hurts and b) your feet (**Füße**) hurt?

4 **Akkupunktur** and **Shiatsu-Massage** – which is **japanisch** and which **chinesisch**?

5 **Magen** means *stomach*, so how do you say in German *She's got stomach ache*?

6 Which one is the odd one out and why: **Kapseln**, **Hustensaft**, **Alkohol**, **Schmerzmittel**, **Tabletten**?

7 If **Alles ist in Ordnung** means *Everything is back to normal*, how would you say *Everything will be back to normal*?

8 What does **Ich kann heute nicht lange reden** mean?

Now check whether you can ...

- say how you're feeling
- list simple symptoms
- explain what hurts when you're in pain
- give information on other people's symptoms
- follow straightforward instructions from a doctor/chemist

When you need to say or understand something in German, it can help to imagine yourself in similar but English-speaking circumstances and think what you'd expect to hear and have to say.

Können Sie das bitte wiederholen is a polite way of asking someone to repeat what he or she has just said. Along with words like **also, na ja**, it's useful if you find you need some thinking time.

Noch mehr! 4

> Verbs which use **sein** in the past include **gebären** (past participle **geboren**) *to be born*; **sterben** (pp **gestorben**) *to die*; **zurückkehren** (pp **zurückgekehrt**) *to return*; **werden** (pp **geworden**) *to become*; **ziehen** (pp **gezogen**) *to move, relocate*; **kommen** (pp **gekommen**) *to come*.
>
> **G20**

1   **Haben oder sein?** Fill the gaps.

a Letzte Woche ...... ich einen Brief an unsere Lokalzeitung geschrieben.

b Meine Tochter und mein Schwiegersohn ...... vor sechs Monaten ein Haus in Leipzig gekauft.

c In den 50er Jahren ...... mein Mann, unsere Kinder und ich nach Australien gezogen.

d Letztes Jahr ...... ich nach Deutschland zurückgekehrt.

e Ich ...... zwei Jahre nach dem Ende des Zweiten Weltkrieges geheiratet.

f Vor vier Jahren ...... mein Mann gestorben.

g Ich heiße Andrea Friedrichsen; ich ...... 1928 in Baden-Baden geboren.

h Gestern ...... der Postbote zwei Antworten auf meinen Brief gebracht.

i Vor zwei Wochen ...... ich mich entschieden, meine alten Klassenkameraden zu suchen.

j Im Jahre 1981 ...... meine Tochter nach Wien gezogen.

> **die Lokalzeitung** *local newspaper* **schreiben** (pp **geschrieben**) *to write* **der Schwiegersohn** *son-in-law* **der Weltkrieg** *world war* **heiraten** *to get married* **eine Antwort** *reply* **bringen** (pp **gebracht**) *to bring* **sich entscheiden** (pp **entschieden**), **... zu suchen** *to decide to search for ...*

2   Reveal Andrea Friedrichsen's life story by arranging the above events in the order they happened and writing a summary in English.

3 Read about Andrea's **Geburtsort** *birthplace* Baden-Baden and fill in the gaps with phrases from the box.

> **Kurtourismus** *spa tourism* **Wasserbehandlung** *hydrotherapy*
> **Kurort** *health resort* **gegründet** *founded*
> **genießen** *to enjoy* **Thermalquellen** *hot springs*

Andrea Friedrichsen wohnt in Baden-Baden, einem populären ...... im Land Baden-Württemberg. Die Römer haben die warmen ...... in dieser Gegend geliebt, und haben circa 80 nach Christus eine Stadt mit vielen Bädern ......

In Deutschland ist der ...... sehr beliebt, und viele Besucher kommen jedes Jahr nach Baden-Baden, und ...... die therapeutischen Qualitäten der ...... mit Temperaturen zwischen 10 und 40 Grad Celsius.

Auf Deutsch

Wo, hier and da/dort are used to describe location when no movement is involved: **Wo sind die Thermalquellen?** *Where are the hot springs?* **Ich wohne hier.** *I live here.* If you're going to somewhere, away from the speaker, the suffix **-hin** is added: **Wohin fährst du?** *Where are you going (to)?* **Fährst du oft dorthin?** *Do you often go there?* If you're coming from somewhere or towards the speaker, the suffix **-her** is added. **Woher kommst du?** *Where do you come from?* **Kommen Sie oft hierher?** *Do you come here often?*

---

4 2•35 Some tourists are asked why they're visiting Baden-Baden. Read the replies and work out what they mean, using the glossary only if necessary. Then listen and note down the last reason you hear, which isn't given below (it begins **Als Kind ...** *As a child ...*).

a Wir kommen aus Norddeutschland. Wir kommen hauptsächlich hierher nach Baden-Baden, weil meine Frau an Arthritis leidet und die Therme sehr gut für sie ist. Wir werden in diesem Jahr auch einen Yoga-Kurs besuchen.

b Wir lieben Wasserbehandlungen, aber wo wir wohnen, gibt es leider keine Thermalquellen. Wir kommen aus diesem Grund jedes Jahr nach Baden-Baden. Dieses Jahr werden wir auch an einem Diätprogramm **teilnehmen** *to take part in*.

c Ich bin hierher gekommen, um Hydrotherapie zu machen. In diesem Jahr werde ich auch Wasseraerobic machen.

d Wir kommen jedes Jahr nach Baden-Baden, weil wir die Behandlungen mögen. Dieses Jahr werden wir auch Fahrräder mieten.

5 The people surveyed mentioned what they do **in diesem Jahr/dieses Jahr** *this year*. Imagine it's a year later and people are reporting back on what they did **letztes Jahr** *last year*, e.g: **Wir werden in diesem Jahr einen Yoga-Kurs besuchen.**
Letztes Jahr habe ich einen Yoga-Kurs besucht.

a Dieses Jahr werden wir an einem Diätprogramm teilnehmen (pp **teilgenommen**).
b Dieses Jahr werden wir Fahrräder mieten.
c In diesem Jahr werde ich Wasseraerobic machen.

6 2•36 Listen to this short podcast on **das Wetter in Baden-Baden** *the weather in Baden-Baden*, which you found posted on a tourist blog about the region. Fill in the missing information.

a Temperature in ...... and ......: around 25°C.
b Temperature in June and September: over ...... °C.
c Temperature at night in ......: between 10 and ...... °C.
d August is the ...... month and ...... is the driest month.
e Temperature in winter: between ...... and ...... °C.
f Weather in winter: ......
g Temperature at ...... in winter: ...... °C.

7 First match the ailments with appropriate remedies from the box, then match the remedies with the instructions on the next page. Use the glossary if you need help with the vocabulary.

a **b** **c**

d **e** **f**

| Magenpulver | Nasenspray | Kopfschmerztabletten |
| Halspastillen | Augentropfen | Erkältungssirup |

1   Nehmen Sie dieses Medikament mit viel Wasser nach dem
    Essen. Überschreiten Sie nicht die Tagesdosis.
2   Geben Sie zwei bis drei Tropfen in das Auge und schließen Sie
    es ein- bis zweimal.
3   Nehmen Sie dreimal täglich zwei 5 ml Löffel.
4   Sprühen Sie zweimal pro Nasenloch, morgens und abends.
5   Lutschen Sie eine oder zwei nach Bedarf.
6   Verrühren Sie dieses Medikament mit 15 ml Wasser und trinken
    Sie die Emulsion vor dem Essen.

8   Read this letter from Georgina Robertson to a guest house in Baden-
    Baden. (**Stattdessen** means *instead*; **bestätigen** means *to confirm*.)

> Sehr geehrte Frau Petzold,
>
> ich habe eine Woche, vom 21. bis 28. April, bei
> Ihnen im Gasthof Zur Krone gebucht. Leider
> muss ich diese Reservierung stornieren, weil mein
> siebzehnjähriger Sohn beim Fußballspiel gefallen ist
> und sein Bein gebrochen hat. Ich kann ihn natürlich
> nicht alleine zu Hause lassen.
>
> Stattdessen möchte ein Freund, Herr Taylor, gerne
> zu Ihnen kommen und hat Ihnen geschrieben, um
> dies zu bestätigen.
>
> Ich bitte um Ihr Verständnis in dieser Angelegenheit.
>
> Mit freundlichen Grüßen
>
> G. Robertson

a   Why is Mrs Robertson *cancelling* (**stornieren**) her booking?
b   Who is Mr Taylor?

9   Write the letter from Mark Taylor to Frau Petzold

    ● saying who you are (name + friend of Mrs Robertson);
    ● explaining that your friend has cancelled her booking and saying why;
    ● stating you'd like to come to the **Gasthof Zur Krone** in her place
      and give the dates.

Mit dem größten Vergnügen!

making suggestions and sending invitations

replying to an invitation

saying what people are like

... and what they look like

In Deutschland ...

not only do people celebrate **Geburtstage** *birthdays* and **Jubiläen** *anniversaries*, but also festivals like **Valentinstag**, **Muttertag** and **Karneval** (the period leading to Lent). On such occasions you'll hear the words **Herzlichen Glückwunsch** *best wishes* and **froh** *happy*: **Herzlichen Glückwunsch zum Geburtstag** *Happy Birthday*, **Frohe Weihnachten** *Happy Christmas*.

Celebrating with a **Grillparty** *barbecue party* or hiring the **Saal** *hall* in a local restaurant, combined with a spot of **Kegeln** *bowling*, are all popular ways of marking an occasion. Many **Kneipen** *pubs* in Germany have their own **Kegelbahn** *bowling alley*.

To accept or decline an invitation, you might use **Danke** or **Tut mir leid** or, more formally, **Mit größtem Vergnügen** or **Es tut uns sehr leid, aber wir werden nicht kommen können.**

Making suggestions and sending invitations

1   The language students are brainstorming ideas for a **Feier** *party* as it is **Claudias Geburtstag** *Claudia's birthday*. Using the glossary, read their suggestions and see if you can work out the German for a) gourmet; b) outside; c) to prepare; d) to invite.

> Ich habe Lust auf (I fancy) eine Grillparty mit Spanferkel!

> Lasst uns (let's) ein Feinschmecker-Abendessen zubereiten!

> Ich schlage vor (I suggest), wir essen im Freien!

> Sollen wir (Shall we) unsere Freunde auf einen Aperitif einladen?

2   As they're on a **Kochkurs** *cookery course* at the **Forsthaus**, they decide on **ein Abendessen**. Pascal sends out invitations to Gesine, on whom he has a crush; one to Julia, a friend of Andreas (the head chef); and one to Boris, a good friend.

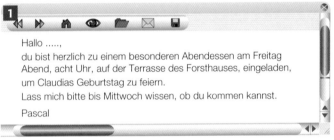

1

Hallo .....,
du bist herzlich zu einem besonderen Abendessen am Freitag Abend, acht Uhr, auf der Terrasse des Forsthauses, eingeladen, um Claudias Geburtstag zu feiern.
Lass mich bitte bis Mittwoch wissen, ob du kommen kannst.

Pascal

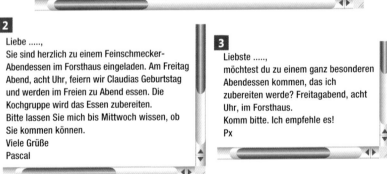

2

Liebe .....,
Sie sind herzlich zu einem Feinschmecker-Abendessen im Forsthaus eingeladen. Am Freitag Abend, acht Uhr, feiern wir Claudias Geburtstag und werden im Freien zu Abend essen. Die Kochgruppe wird das Essen zubereiten.
Bitte lassen Sie mich bis Mittwoch wissen, ob Sie kommen können.
Viele Grüße
Pascal

3

Liebste .....,
möchtest du zu einem ganz besonderen Abendessen kommen, das ich zubereiten werde? Freitagabend, acht Uhr, im Forsthaus.
Komm bitte. Ich empfehle es!
Px

a   Who gets which invitation?
b   When and where is the **Abendessen** to take place?

Replying to an invitation

DAS FORSTHAUS

Landhaus aus dem achtzehnten Jahrhundert im Grünen
Saal; Kegelbahn
KURSE für ERWACHSENE in
Malen und Zeichnen • Naturfotografie • Heilkräuterkunde
Weinprobe lokaler Weine • traditionelles Kochen

3 **2•37** Listen to the key language:

Mit (dem größten) Vergnügen!	I'd love to! *Lit.* with (the greatest) pleasure.
Die Feier wird ... stattfinden.	The party will take place ...
Wie schade!	What a pity!
Danke für die Einladung.	Thanks for the invitation.
Ich weiß nicht, ob ich kann.	I don't know if I can.
Hast du Lust, ... zu ...?	Do you feel like ...?

4 **2•38** Guido's job is to phone Nico, Jan and Katharina. Listen and match the answers to the people.

- **Tut mir leid, aber am Freitag können wir nicht kommen. Wie schade!**
- **Was für eine nette Idee. Mit Vergnügen!**
- **Ja, ich komme mit dem größten Vergnügen! Herzlichen Dank.**

5 **2•39** Listen to a phone message from Fabian and decide why he can't come to the party.

6 **2•40** Pascal rings Gesine to see if she got his e-mail – **Hast du meine E-Mail erhalten?**
Is she going to come to the dinner or not?

Saying what people are like

1 2•41 Listen to the key language:

Kennst du Gesine?	Do you know Gesine?
Ich weiß (es) nicht.	I don't know.
Warum weißt du es nicht?	How come you don't know?
Ich kenne sie nicht gut.	I don't know her well.
Er ist so sympathisch.	He's so nice.
Ich stimme dir (nicht) zu.	I (don't) agree with you.

There are two words for *to know*: **kennen**: to know people or places; **wissen**: to know things or facts. **Wissen** is irregular:

ich	weiß	wir	wissen
du	weißt	ihr	wisst
er/sie/es	weiß	sie/Sie	wissen

Es *it* is often included with **wissen** in German even though it's not needed in English: **Ich weiß es nicht.** *I don't know (it).*

2 2•42 Listen to Pascal and Guido talking about Gesine, then fill the gaps in their conversation with **kann, weißt, weiß** (x 2).

Guido	**Kommt Gesine zum Abendessen?**
Pascal	**Ich ...... es nicht.**
Guido	**Warum ...... du es nicht?**
Pascal	**Ich habe gesagt, ich ...... nicht, ob sie kommen ......**
Guido	**Wie unfreundlich!**

3 2•43 Poor Pascal gets an **SMS** *text* from Gesine saying **komme Frei nicht** *not coming Fri*. Listen to Guido's conversation with Christine and write **P** next to the adjectives referring to Pascal and **G** next to those referring to Gesine.

fröhlich *cheerful*	**lieb** *kind, sweet*
enttäuscht *disappointed*	**lustig** *funny, amusing*
höflich *polite*	**nett** *nice*
unhöflich *rude*	**unfreundlich** *unfriendly*
gemein *mean*	**sympathisch** *pleasant*
gut *good*	**sanft** *gentle*

Do they agree about Gesine's character?

... and what they look like

4 2•44 Listen to the key language:

Ich habe eine Nachricht erhalten.	I received a message.
Wer ist er/sie?	Who is he/she?
Wie sieht er/sie aus?	What does he/she look like?
Sie ist dunkelhaarig/blond.	She's dark-haired/blonde.
Sie ist schlank/mollig.	She's slim/chubby.
Sie ist 1.75m groß.	She's 1.75m tall.
Sie lächelt immer.	She's always smiling.

5 2•45 Christine's doing some subtle matchmaking by talking to Pascal about Gudrun from the photography course. Listen and decide:

- whether Gudrun is: dark   blonde   slim   chubby
- how tall she is ....

Doch is used to contradict a negative statement or question:

Ich kenne sie nicht. – Doch, du kennst sie!
Du kommst nicht zur Party, oder? – Doch, ich komme!

---

6 2•46 Christine tries to jog Pascal's memory by describing Gudrun's eyes and **Haar** *hair*. Listen and decide:

- whether Gudrun's eyes are:
  blau *blue*   **braun** *brown*   **grün** *green*   **hellbraun** *light brown*

- and whether her hair is:
  glatt *straight*   **lockig** *curly*   **lang** *long*   **kurz** *short*

7 2•47 Later Christine asks Guido whether Boris has replied: **Hat Boris geantwortet**? Listen then say in English what Boris looks like.

New phrases to look out for are:

Der kleine, dicke Typ ... *The short, fat bloke ...*
... mit einem Schnäuzer. *... with a moustache.*
Er ist weder dick noch dünn. *He's neither fat nor thin.*
Er kleidet sich sportlich. *He dresses casually.*
Er ist atemberaubend gutaussehend. *He's breathtakingly good-looking.*

---

put it all together

1 You're planning to go out. Make these suggestions in German.

   a Let's go to the restaurant.
   b Shall we eat outside?
   c Let's go to the disco!
   d I fancy the pub.
   e Shall we go to Berlin tomorrow?
   f I suggest we go wine tasting (**eine Weinprobe machen**).
   g I fancy the theatre (**das Theater**).

2 Say what these words mean and give their opposites.

   klein   **kurz**   **höflich**   **dünn**   **blond**
   unsympathisch **schlank**   **unfreundlich**

3 Here's an invitation to celebrate a **Hochzeitstag** *wedding anniversary*. Fill the gaps with the words in the box.

haben	**gehen**	**feiern**	**eingeladen**	**lasst**

   > Liebe Freunde,
   > ihr seid herzlich zu einer Feier am Samstag, den 16. Juni,
   > .... Wir ..... ein Abendessen im Restaurant
   > Zum Stadttor, in der Kirchhofstraße organisiert, um
   > unseren Hochzeitstag zu ...... Danach ..... wir in die
   > Diskothek in der Kastanienallee. Bitte ..... uns bis zum
   > 31. Mai wissen, ob ihr kommen könnt.
   > Liebe Grüße
   > Ramona und Paul

4 Write a similar letter to a friend, Tim, inviting him to a party
   to celebrate your birthday on Friday October 12th. Tell him
   you've organised a dinner at the Gasthof Meistertrunk at eight
   o'clock in the evening, and ask him to reply by September 30th.

5 How would Tim reply a) thanking you for the invitation,
   saying it's a lovely idea and he'd love to come; b) apologising
   and saying it's a pity; he can't come because he's going on
   holiday?

now you're talking!

1 2•48 A colleague's telling you about Marlene – but you've absolutely no idea who she's talking about.

- **Weißt du, dass Marlene nicht zur Konferenz geht?**
- ◆ Say you don't know Marlene.
- **Doch, du kennst sie. Sie arbeitet mit Georg und Lavinia.**
- ◆ Ask what she looks like; is she tall?
- **Also... nein, sie ist weder groß noch klein. Zirka ein Meter siebzig. Sie hat lockiges Haar und braune Augen.**
- ◆ Ask if she's blonde. Slim?
- **Blond, ja. Und ziemlich schlank.**
- ◆ You've realised who she is. Say yes, you know Marlene, she's really nice.
- **Sympathisch? Marlene? Ich glaube, sie ist nicht sehr sympathisch.**

2 2•49 Your friend Armin phones to say it's ages since he's seen you and to invite you out to celebrate his birthday.

- **Hallo. Wir haben uns schon lange nicht gesehen! Hör mal, ich möchte gerne mit dir ausgehen, um meinen Geburtstag zu feiern.**
- ◆ Say it's a great idea; you'd love to.
- **Also, ich habe geplant, wir gehen am Dienstag in die Diskothek in der Kirchhofstraße.**
- ◆ Say you're sorry, you can't on Tuesday because you're going to Tübingen.
- **Oh je, wie schade! Aber hör mal, ich möchte zu Martas Geburtstagsfeier gehen. Sie wird am 3. Dezember stattfinden. Möchtest du auch kommen?**
- ◆ Say thanks a lot, you'd love to. Wish him a happy birthday and send greetings to Marta (**Grüße an Marta**).

3 2•50 **Wie sieht Leo aus?** Without any prompts, describe Leo, who's breathtakingly good-looking: he's dark haired, has brown eyes is 1.8m tall and dresses casually.

quiz

1 Which is the odd one out here: **Geburtstag, Glückwunsch, Schnäuzer, Feier, Jubiläum?**

2 If you receive a text message saying **mit größtem Vergnügen**, has your invitation been accepted or declined?

3 What's the German for a wine tasting?

4 What's the difference in meaning between **die Feier hat am Samstag stattgefunden** and **die Feier wird am Samstag stattfinden?**

5 Would you use **ich weiß sie nicht** or **ich kenne sie nicht** to say you don't know somebody's phone number?

6 How would you say you feel like doing something: **ich habe Angst, ich habe Lust** or **ich habe Hunger?**

Now check whether you can ...

- make a suggestion
- send an invitation
- accept an invitation
- refuse politely, apologising and giving a reason
- describe somebody physically
- describe somebody's character

Put your learning into practice by seeing if you can describe someone, be it your nearest and dearest or someone from a magazine.
Double the impact of what you've just learnt by putting **sehr, ein bisschen, ziemlich, so** or **total** before the adjective. Try comparing people, using adjectives with an **-er** ending and **als: Marlene ist größer als Marta** *Marlene's taller than Maria.*

Ein lieblicher Weißwein

following a recipe

choosing wine to complement a dish

commenting on a meal

expressing your appreciation

In Deutschland ...

Kartoffeln *potatoes* are a staple which appear in many guises on the German plate. Another firm favourite is the **Knödel** or **Kloß** *dumpling*, depending on the region. These come in all varieties and are even served as desserts.

Most vineyards are found in the south-west, along the River Rhine. Due to Germany's climate, mainly white wine is produced. However, there are some good red wines, notably the **Spätburgunder** or **Dornfelder**.

Look out for the label: **Qualitätswein b.A.** (**bestimmter Anbaugebiete** *from selected wine-growing areas*) or **Qualitätswein mit Prädikat**, which guarantees the origin and quality of the wine. And don't forget, to toast you say: **Prost**, **Prosit**, or **Zum Wohl**.

Following a recipe

Brötchen   Petersilie *parsley* Zwiebel   Eier

1 These are words often found in recipes:

geben *to put* (lit. *to give*)	**braten** *to fry*
kochen *to cook/boil*	**erwärmen** *to heat*
schneiden *to cut*	**Stückchen** *small pieces*
gießen *to pour*	**der Teig** *dough*
vermischen *to mix*	**kochend** *boiling*
auseinanderfallen *to fall apart*	**nass** *wet*

Auf Deutsch

Folgen *to follow*, like **helfen** *to help*, **danken** *to thank* and **gratulieren** *to congratulate*, is followed by the dative: **Sie müssen dem Rezept folgen**.

G4

2 2•51 Andreas, **der Chefkoch** at the **Forsthaus**, is demonstrating how to cook **den perfekten Knödel**. Put the instructions in the correct order and then listen to check your answers. **Fertig?** *Ready?*

A Schneiden Sie sechs alte Brötchen in Stückchen.

B Braten Sie eine gehackte Zwiebel und etwas Petersilie in Butter. Vermischen Sie dann alles mit den Brötchenstücken.

C Formen Sie mit nassen Händen tennisballgroße Knödel.

D Es ist nicht schwierig, Knödel zu kochen, wenn Sie dem Rezept gut folgen.

E Vermischen Sie drei Eier mit Pfeffer und Salz und gießen Sie sie über den Teig.

F Geben Sie die Knödel in heißes, aber nicht kochendes Wasser, weil die Knödel sonst auseinanderfallen. Das ist eine goldene Regel!

G Nach 20 Minuten sind die Knödel fertig – guten Appetit!

H Erwärmen Sie etwas Milch und gießen Sie sie über den Brötchenteig.

3 2•51 Listen again, then read the transcript on page 126. According to Andreas, what's the golden rule for making **Knödel**?

Choosing wine to complement a dish

1 2•52 Listen to the key language:

passende Weine zu den Gängen	matching wines with the courses
nach Geschmack	according to taste
Wird der Wein .... serviert?	Is the wine served ...?
kalt	cold
auf Raumtemperatur	at room temperature
Was wird .... getrunken?	What is drunk ...?

2 These are the dishes for the **Feinschmecker-Abendessen**. Check the meaning of any new words and label each dish **Vorspeise, Hauptspeise or Nachspeise**.

> **Apfelstrudel mit Sahne**
> **Champignoncremesuppe**
> **Schweinebraten mit gerösteten Frühkartoffeln und Rotkohl**

3 2•53 While the others are putting the finishing touches to the meal, Guido tells Andreas about their choice of drinks. Listen and decide which of these drinks goes with which course.

Apfelwein	Gewürztraminer	Bier
Trockenbeerenauslese	Weißherbst	
Dornfelder	Sekt	

4 2•53 Listen again to Guido and Andreas then choose from the list below the adjectives used to describe each of these wines: **Sekt, Weißherbst, Gewürztraminer, Dornfelder, Trockenbeerenauslese**.

weiß *white*	**ausgereift** *aged*
rosé *rosé*	**leicht** *light*
rot *red*	**trocken** *dry*
halbtrocken *semi-dry*	**fruchtig** *fruity*
lieblich *sweet*	**vollmundig** *full-bodied*
jung *young*	**elegant** *elegant*

Werden with a past participle is used to say that something is done:

<u>Das Wasser</u> wird gekocht. *The water is boiled.*
<u>Die Eier</u> werden vermischt. *The eggs are mixed.*

Auf Deutsch

Commenting on a meal

1 **2•54** Listen to the key language:

Hast du ... probiert?	Did you taste/try ...?
Hat Ihnen ... geschmeckt?	Did you like ...?
perfekt zubereitet	cooked to perfection
Sie ist mir ein bisschen ...	It's (f) a bit ... for me.
zu salzig/süß	too salty/sweet
Die Suppe schmeckt ...	The soup tastes ...
Er enthält ...	It (m) contains ...
Es erinnert mich an ...	It reminds me of ...

2 **2•55** Before you listen to snatches of conversation heard during the **Abendessen**, see if you can match the two halves of each one.

a Möchtest du den Weißwein probieren?	**1** Er hat mir sehr gut geschmeckt – perfekt zubereitet!
b Dieser Rotwein ist sehr gut.	**2** Sie ist mir ein bisschen zu salzig.
c Hat Ihnen der Schweinebraten geschmeckt?	**3** Perfekt! Ich glaube, er enthält Rum, oder?
d Was hältst du von dem Apfelstrudel?	**4** Mm ... trocken, leicht, delikat ... er hat einen eleganten Geschmack.
e Hast du die Champignoncremesuppe probiert?	**5** Er ist wirklich vollmundig!

3 **2•56** Listen to Andreas and his friend Julia discussing the Apfelstrudel and decide who used to make one like it and when.

Wer? ....   Wann? ....

> To express *used to*, you add **früher** to the perfect or imperfect tense:
>
> **Früher hat sie einen Apfelstrudel gebacken.** *She used to make an apple strudel.*
>
> **Wir haben früher den Apfelstrudel mit Vanillesoße gegessen.** *We used to eat the apple strudel with custard.*

Auf Deutsch

Expressing your appreciation

1 **2•57** Listen to the key language:

Herzlichen Dank.	Thank you so much.
Es bereitet mir große Freude.	It gives me great pleasure.
Kompliment an den Chefkoch /die Köche.	Compliments to the head chef/the cooks.
Es ist ausgezeichnet gelaufen.	It went superbly.
Wir hatten so viel Spaß.	We had so much fun.
nicht nur … sondern auch …	not only … but also …
Wir werden wiederkommen.	We'll come back.

2 **2•58** At the end of the **Abendessen**, Andreas makes a speech and wishes someone a happy birthday. Listen and pick out:

a what word he uses to describe the **Abendessen**;
b which course he feels was a **Meisterwerk** *masterpiece*;
c to whom he proposes **einen Toast**;
d to whom he wishes a happy birthday.

3 On behalf of the cookery class, Pascal writes a thank-you note to Andreas. They've learnt **eine Menge** *a lot* of things – which three are mentioned in the letter?

Lieber Andreas,

herzlichen Dank für alles. Der Kochkurs war fantastisch, wir hatten so viel Spaß und haben eine Menge gelernt. Wir haben nicht nur gelernt, wie man ein deutsches Essen zubereitet, sondern auch wie man den passenden Wein wählt. Und: wir haben sehr viel Deutsch gelernt!

Kurzum – es war fantastisch! Wir werden wiederkommen!

Liebe Grüße von der Klasse von 2012.

Pascal, Guido, Christine, Mel

put it all together

1   Match the words with their meanings.

a	probieren	1	ein kleiner Teil/ein kleines Stück
b	Geburtstag	2	zwischen fünf und acht Grad
c	geröstet	3	ein Gemüse
d	Apfelstrudel	4	nur ein bisschen essen oder trinken
e	Stückchen	5	der Tag, an dem man geboren ist
f	passend	6	eine Nachspeise
g	kalt	7	das, was für die Situation am besten ist
h	Rotkohl	8	im Ofen zubereitet

2   Rearrange these instructions to find a recipe for an omelette –
you'll need a **Pfanne** *frying pan*. **Schmelzen** means *to melt*.

Ein einfaches Omelett für zwei Personen:

a   Geben Sie die Eier in die Pfanne.

b   Vermischen Sie die Eier mit Pfeffer, Salz und etwas
Wasser.

c   Zuerst schmelzen Sie zehn Gramm Butter.

d   Servieren Sie es sofort.

e   Nehmen Sie das Omelett aus der Pfanne.

f   Lassen Sie alles zwei Minuten kochen.

3   Which tenses are these verbs?

ich	imperfect	perfect	present	future
werde kochen				
habe geschlafen				
hatte				
rufe … an				
bin gegangen				
wohne				
werde arbeiten				
habe gegessen				
werde beenden				
war				
habe geglaubt				

now you're talking!

1 **2•59** Take part in the general chatter during a party with neighbours in Germany. Your neighbours made and brought a large pot of **Erbsensuppe** *pea soup* – a thick stew-type dish made from dried peas, potatoes and meat. They also brought a range of different types of bread. You know most of them well enough to use **du**.

- ● **Schmeckt dir die Erbsensuppe?**
- ◆ Say it's superb – cooked to perfection.
- ● **Du musst diese Mohnbrötchen** *poppy-seed rolls* **probieren. Sie schmecken so gut.**
- ◆ Say yes, they're very good, and ask if he's tasted the **Sesam** rolls.
- ● **Die Sesambrötchen schmecken mir am besten. Aber dieses Brot hier ist auch gut ... Und was hältst du von dem Wein?** *What do you think of the wine?*
- ◆ Comment that it's superb, so light and fruity. Say you like it.
- ● **Die deutschen Weine sind gut, nicht wahr?**
- ◆ Say you really liked the aperitif, the **Sekt**.

2 **2•60** You go to talk to your neighbour's grandmother.

- ◆ As she's done much of the cooking, say *What a beautiful cake* **Kuchen** (m).
- ● **Ich habe ihn nach einem Rezept meiner Großmutter gebacken. Er enthält Mandeln. Sind Sie allergisch gegen Nüsse** *nuts*?
- ◆ Work out how to say you're not allergic to nuts.
- ● **Was halten Sie von dem Kuchen?**
- ◆ You taste a piece, say you like it a lot and that it reminds you of an English recipe. Say *Compliments to the head chef!*
- ● **Morgen gebe ich Ihnen das Rezept.**
- ◆ It's time to go, so thank your neighbour, Fabian, say you've enjoyed yourself so much and say goodbye.
- ● **Auf Wiedersehen.**

quiz

1 What's the missing word in this sentence? **Geben Sie die Knödel in heißes, aber nicht kochendes, ...**

2 Is *to taste* **schmecken** or **vermischen**?

3 Which is the odd one out: **leicht, lieblich, vollmundig, geröstet**?

4 How would you say *The wine is not only light but also fruity?*

5 What's the best translation for *I used to cook a lot* – **Gestern habe ich viel gekocht** or **Früher habe ich viel gekocht**?

6 Is **Dornfelder** a red or a white wine?

7 How would you say *the soup is cooked*?

8 How would you say *Compliments to the head chef*?

Now check whether you can ...

- understand some of the key words used in recipes
- choose a German wine to complement certain foods
- comment on a meal, giving praise or saying what you're not fond of
- say you're allergic to something
- thank your host and express your appreciation
- follow formal instructions

When you're speaking a new language it's normal to forget words and to be put off your stride as you struggle for the right word. If it happens to you, don't grind to a halt, but try to explain what you want to say using different words. You've seen how this works on page 100 – now have a go yourself at getting round these: **braten, Kartoffelknödel, Dornfelder, lieblich, ausgezeichnet**.

Noch mehr! 5

■ Lübeck: die Stadt des Marzipans

Schleswig-Holstein ist das nördlichste Bundesland Deutschlands. Von Berlin kann man die Landeshauptstadt Hamburg mit der Berlin-Hamburg Bahn, die bis zu 190 km/h schnell fährt, in ungefähr 100 Minuten erreichen.

Etwa 65 km südwestlich von Hamburg befindet sich Lübeck. Wegen seiner geografischen Lage wird es auch das „Tor zum Norden" genannt. Lübeck ist eine Hafenstadt. Der Lübecker Hafen ist der größte Ostseehafen in Deutschland. Seit 1987 wurden Teile des mittelalterlichen Altstadtkerns zum UNESCO Weltkulturerbe erklärt.

Die Firma Niederegger existiert seit 1806 und ist weltbekannt für ihr Lübecker Marzipan. Hier findet man auch das Marzipanmuseum.

Ca. 20 km von der Lübecker Altstadt findet man Travemünde, ein elegantes Ostseeheilbad, wo es viel zu tun und zu sehen gibt.

You can make the name of a town into an adjective by adding -er. The ending never changes: **die Berliner Mauer** *The Berlin Wall*; **das Wiener Schnitzel**. The same words can be used for people, with -in added for a female: **Er ist Berliner/sie ist Berlinerin**.

Auf Deutsch

1   Richtig oder falsch?

		richtig	falsch
a	Schleswig-Holstein befindet sich in Norddeutschland.	☐	☐
b	Von Berlin ist man in unter einer Stunde in Hamburg, wenn man mit der Berlin-Hamburg Bahn fährt.	☐	☐
c	Lübeck liegt südwestlich von Hamburg.	☐	☐
d	Lübeck ist die Hauptstadt von Schleswig-Holstein.	☐	☐
e	Der Hafen in Lübeck ist der größte Hafen der Welt.	☐	☐
f	Lübeck ist die Heimat des Lübecker Marzipans.	☐	☐
g	In Lübeck gibt es auch ein Marzipanmuseum.	☐	☐
h	Travemünde ist in der Nähe von Lübeck.	☐	☐

2 Rob und Samira Nelson aus Durham in Nordengland möchten ihr Haus mit einer Familie in Schleswig-Holstein tauschen. Hier beschreiben sie ihr Haus.

New-build detached house: hall, cloakroom, sitting room with fireplace and French windows leading to patio, study/fourth bedroom, fully equipped family kitchen, utility room. Master bedroom with ensuite, two further bedrooms, family bathroom. Gas central heating. Double garage, garden to rear with open aspect to golf course. Good proximity to shops, schools, station, resturants and municipal swimming pool.

Füllen Sie dieses Formular für die Familie Nelson mit ✓ und ✗ aus. Schreiben Sie ?, wenn die Informationen fehlen (lit. *are missing*).

Land, in dem sich das Haus befindet [   ]

Immobilientyp [   ]

Anzahl der Schlafzimmer [   ] **Anzahl der Badezimmer** ☐

Merkmale der Immobilie:

Garten	☐	Garage/Stellplatz	☐
Terrasse	☐	Panoramablick	☐
Balkon	☐	Privatpool	☐
Klimaanlage	☐	Zentralheizung	☐

Ausstattung:

moderne Küche	☐	Spülmaschine	☐
Fernseher	☐	Internetanschluss	☐
Aufzug	☐	Kamin	☐

In der Nähe:

Geschäfte	☐	Restaurants	☐
Strand	☐	Spielplatz	☐
öffentliches Schwimmbad	☐	öffentliche Transportmittel	☐
Sportzentrum	☐	Golfplatz	☐

3   **a**   **2•61 Herr und Frau Nelson haben ihr Haus mit der Familie Retzlaff, die in der Nähe von Lübeck wohnt, getauscht. Elke Ehlers wohnt im Nachbarhaus. Sie sind Rob Nelson in der folgenden Konversation.**

- **Willkommen in Deutschland. Ich heiße Elke.**
- ◆ Say you're pleased to meet her and introduce yourself. Tell her your wife's not here, she's gone into town.
- **Wie heißt Ihre Frau?**
- ◆ Answer her question.
- **Gefällt Ihnen Schleswig-Holstein?**
- ◆ Say you like it a lot – it's so beautiful and interesting.
- **Sind Sie zum ersten Mal in Deutschland?**
- ◆ Say you (i.e. both of you) were in Berlin two years ago. Last year you went to France – but you prefer Germany. Add that you personally just love Germany; you've been studying German for two years.

b   **2•62 Nach einer Woche lädt Elke die Nelsons zum Abendessen ein.**

- **Also, was haben Sie bis jetzt** *until now* **in Schleswig-Holstein gesehen?**
- ◆ Say that on Monday – on your own – you went to Lübeck where you saw the Holstentor. You really liked it.
- **Wie war das Wetter?**
- ◆ Say it was hot.
- **Wann sind Sie abgefahren** *leave***?**
- ◆ Tell her you left at eight o'clock in the morning.
- **Und was haben Sie am Dienstag gemacht?**
- ◆ Say you (both) went to Travemünde where you visited the Seebadmuseum Travemünde.
- **Haben Sie das Maritim Hochhaus gesehen?**
- ◆ Say yes, you saw it but, unfortunately, you have no photos because you lost your **Kamera**.
- **Wie schade! Haben Sie eine Anzeige gemacht?**
- ◆ Say yes, you went to the police station in Lübeck.
- **Noch ein Glas Wein, Rob?**
- ◆ It's getting late so say *no, thank you*. Say you've enjoyed yourselves very much but you have to leave. Thank Elke.
- **Bitte – keine Ursache! Bis nächstes Jahr!**

4 Write a card to your friend Maria in Berlin as if you were Samira, using your diary as a prompt. Finish off by saying that the holiday has been wonderful and you'll be back in Germany next year. (*To stay* is **wohnen**).

Sat	Arrived Germany, staying in big detached house near Lübeck. Supermarket nearby + small pub
Sun	V. hot; get up early every day.
Mon	R & I went to Lübeck, R saw Holstentor, I bought a pile of things!
Tue	Fantastic view here. However, no photos – today p.m. R lost camera. Reported it at police station, filled in form, then took the wrong street and got back after 12 p.m!

Liebe Maria,

Bravo! You've completed *Talk German 2* and should now have a broad enough grasp of the structures of German to cope in everyday situations without being restricted to set phrases.

Don't expect to remember everything you've learnt. Many people find they need to revisit things several times before they really sink in. So go back occasionally, reading and listening to the units again.

The one really important thing to do is to use your German. Whenever you can, talk to people and listen to German, read anything you can lay your hands on and write things down.

transcripts and answers

Unit 1

Page 8

2 ● Wie heißt du?
  ◆ Ich heiße **Stefanie Zimmermann.**
  ● Bist du Deutsche?
  ◆ Ja, natürlich.
  ● Wo wohnst du?
  ◆ Ich wohne mit meiner Familie in **Bad Krotzingen, in der Nähe von Freiburg.**
  Her name is Stefanie; she lives in Bad Krotzingen, near Freiburg.

3 ● Hallo, ich **heiße** Tom.
  ◆ Freut mich. **Bist** du Engländer?
  ● Nein, ich **bin** Amerikaner. Und du? Wie **heißt** du?
  ◆ Eva.
  ● Woher **kommst** du?
  ◆ Ich **komme** aus Warschau in Polen. Ich bin Polin, aber ich **wohne** in Deutschland.
  ● Und ich wohne **mit** meinem Bruder in England, in der Nähe **von** Bristol.

Page 9

2 ● Darf ich Eva vorstellen? Sie ist Polin, sie kommt aus Warschau in Polen. Sie wohnt in Deutschland.
  ◆ Er heißt Tom. Er ist Amerikaner, aber er wohnt nicht in Amerika – er wohnt mit seinem Bruder in England, in der Nähe von Bristol.

3 ● Bist du verheiratet?
  ◆ **Ja, mein Mann heißt Ulrich.**
  ● Hast du Kinder?
  ◆ **Ja, wir haben zwei. Sie heißen Michael und Sabine.**
  ● Wie alt sind sie?
  ◆ **Michael ist acht Jahre alt.**
  ● Und wie alt ist Sabine?
  ◆ **Vier. Sie ist vier Jahre alt.**
  a richtig; b falsch; c falsch; d falsch; e falsch
  b Ihr Mann heißt Ulrich; c Sie haben zwei Kinder; d Ihre Tochter heißt Sabine; e Ihre Tochter ist vier Jahre alt.

Page 10

2 *a* Ärztin (doctor); *b* Klempner (plumber); *c* Tischler (carpenter); *d* Journalistin (journalist); *e* Kellner (waiter); *f* Friseurin (hairdresser); *g* Buchhalter (accountant); *h* Redakteurin (editor)

  ● Was bist du von Beruf?
  ◆ Ich bin Ärztin von Beruf. Und du, was bist du von Beruf?
  ● Ich bin Klempner. Was bist du von Beruf?
  ◆ Ich bin Journalist. Ich arbeite von zuhause. Was bist du von Beruf?
  ● Ich bin Friseurin, und ich arbeite abends als Kellnerin. Und du?
  ◆ Ich arbeite als Buchhalter bei Siemens. Und was bist du von Beruf?
  ● Ich bin Tischler.

3 ● Ich arbeite für eine Fluggesellschaft. Ich bin seit 2002 Pressesprecherin.
  ◆ Ich bin seit dreizehn Jahren Immobilienmakler.
  a since 2002; b 13 years

Page 11

2 ● Warum lernst du Deutsch?
  ◆ Weil ich Sprachen mag.
  ● Und du?
  ◆ Ich möchte in Österreich arbeiten.
  ● Und du, Anna?
  ◆ Ich möchte deutsche Bücher lesen.
  ● Und du, warum bist du hier?
  ◆ Ich mag die deutsche Kultur.
  ● Warum lernst du Deutsch?
  ◆ Weil ich Deutschland liebe!
  ● Und ihr?
  ◆ Ich mag das deutsche Bier.
  ● Ich höre gern Opernmusik.
  ◆ Aus Neugier – das ist alles!
  a 6; b 2; c 8; d 5; e 4; f 9; g 3; h 7; i 1
  ***Ich reise sehr gern** is not mentioned.*

3 ● Joan, warum möchtest du Deutsch lernen?
  ◆ Ich möchte mit meiner Schwiegertochter sprechen. Sie ist Deutsche.

- Woher kommt sie?
- ◆ Sie kommt aus Frankfurt. Sie heißt Angelika.

Her name is Angelika and she's from Frankfurt.

Page 12 Put it all together

1 *a* 2; *b* 6; *c* 5; *d* 7; *e* 1; *f* 4; *g* 3

2 ich trinke, er/sie/es trinkt, wir trinken, sie/Sie trinken; du machst, er/sie/es macht, ihr macht, sie/Sie machen; ich zahle, du zahlst, wir zahlen, ihr zahlt

3 *a* Ich heiße Robert Meister. Ich bin siebenunddreißig Jahre alt und bin Deutscher. Ich wohne seit fünfzehn Jahren in Bremen. Ich bin seit acht Jahren Grafiker von Beruf.

b Darf ich Robert Meister vorstellen? Er ist siebenunddreißig Jahre alt und ist Deutscher. Er wohnt seit fünfzehn Jahren in Bremen. Er ist seit acht Jahren Grafiker von Beruf.

Page 13 Now you're talking!

1 ● Hallo! Wie heißt du?
- **◆ Ich heiße Christine Carpenter.**
- ● Bist du Amerikanerin?
- **◆ Nein, ich bin Engländerin.**
- ● Woher in England kommst du?
- **◆ Aus Brighton.**
- ● Was bist du von Beruf?
- **◆ Ich bin Fotografin von Beruf.**
- ● Seit wann bist du Fotografin?
- **◆ Ich bin seit sieben Jahren Fotografin.**
- ● Warum möchtest du Deutsch lernen?
- **◆ Weil ich gern reise.**

2 ● **Hallo. Wie heißt du?**
- ◆ Jürgen – Jürgen Donner. Freut mich.
- ● **Woher kommst du?**
- ◆ Ich komme aus Köln.
- ● **Wohnst du in Köln?**
- ◆ Nein. Ich wohne seit 2008 in Lübeck.
- ● **Was bist du von Beruf?**
- ◆ Ich bin Grafiker. Ich arbeite von zuhause, weil ich eine kleine Tochter habe.

- ● **Wie alt ist sie?**
- ◆ Sie ist vierzehn Monate alt und sehr süß.

Page 14 Quiz

1 using du; 2 Darf ich Klaus vorstellen?; 3 e; 4 ist; 5 Klempnerin; 6 seit; 7 Ich reise gern; 8 languages

Unit 2
Pages 16 & 17

2 ● Es gibt einen Flug **um siebzehn Uhr zwanzig** nach Berlin, aber er ist voll; es gibt leider keine Plätze mehr.
- ◆ Und der nächste Flug?
- ● Der nächste Flug geht um **neunzehn Uhr dreißig** und ein anderer geht um **einundzwanzig Uhr vierzehn.**
- ◆ Gibt es einen Flug vor **siebzehn Uhr**?
- ● Nein, leider nicht.
17.20; 19.30; 21.14

3 ● Hier ist der Anrufbeantworter von Martin Droste. Bitte hinterlassen Sie eine Nachricht nach dem Zeichen.
- ◆ Guten Tag, Herr Droste. Hier spricht Ricardo Silva. Mein Flug kommt um **zwanzig Uhr fünfundreißig** in Berlin an.
20.35

4 Ich **komme um achtzehn Uhr fünfundzwanzig an.**

5 rufen, an

7 **Um Viertel nach zehn** (10.15) beginnen wir mit dem Vortrag des Ministers zum Klimawandel. **Um Viertel vor elf** (10.45) treffen wir die anderen europäischen Delegierten, und dann diskutieren wir das Thema Klimawandel. **Um halb zwölf** (11.30) machen wir eine Kaffeepause, und dann sprechen wir mit dem Minister bis zum Mittagessen **um ein Uhr** (1.00). Nach dem Mittagessen besichtigen wir eine Firma für Umwelttechnik. **Um sieben Uhr** (7.00) gehen alle Delegierten in ein Restaurant, und **um halb acht** (7.30) essen wir zusammen zu Abend.

Pages 18 & 19

2 *a* Ich wache um acht Uhr auf.
b Ich trainiere um halb neun im Fitnessstudio.
c Normalerweise dusche ich mich um Viertel nach acht.
d Ich stehe um Viertel vor sieben auf.
e Ich entspanne mich um elf Uhr abends.
f Ich ziehe mich so gegen zehn nach sechs an.
b 4; *d* 5; *c* 1; *f* 2; *e* 3; *a* 6

3 ● Ich wache früh auf – so gegen halb sieben und normalerweise stehe ich um sieben Uhr auf. Ich dusche mich und ziehe mich an. Manchmal trainiere ich nach der Arbeit im Fitnessstudio. Es ist in der Nähe von meinem Büro. Dann gehe ich nach Hause und entspanne mich. So gegen halb elf gehe ich ins Bett.
He gets up at 07.00; He showers and gets dressed; he sometimes works out at the gym near his office after work; He goes home and relaxes.

5 ● Anja, um wieviel Uhr stehst du auf?
◆ Ich stehe um acht Uhr auf, aber Martin steht um sieben Uhr auf. Ich dusche mich um halb neun. Ich arbeite von zuhause – ich bin Webdesignerin – aber Martin pendelt. Er arbeitet in Mannheim. Er verlässt das Haus um sieben Uhr fünfundzwanzig. Abends geht Martin ins Fitnessstudio und trainiert. Dann geht er nach Hause und wir essen um acht Uhr zu Abend. Normalerweise sehe ich am Abend fern.
a M; *b* A; *c* A; *d* M; *e* M; *f* M; *g* M & A; *h* A.

6 Um wieviel Uhr wachst/stehst du auf?; er/sie wacht/steht um … auf; wir wachen/stehen um … auf

Page 20 Put it all together

1 *a* 4; *b* 5; *c* 7; *d* 6; *e* 2; *f* 1; *g* 3

2 *b* um halb acht morgens; *c* um Viertel nach vier nachmittags; *d* um zwanzig nach sechs morgens; *e* um elf Uhr abends

3 *a* arbeitet; *b* beginnt; *c* arbeiten; *d* stehen auf; *e* trainiere; *f* stehe, auf, dusche, mich, ziehe, an

4 Normalerweise wache ich früh auf. Dann stehe ich um halb acht auf und verlasse das Haus um acht Uhr. Ich pendle; ich gehe um sieben Uhr abends nach Hause, sehe fern, esse zu Abend und manchmal gehe ich um elf Uhr ins Bett.

Page 21 Now you're talking!

1 ● Michael, wo wohnst du?
◆ **Ich wohne in Cheshire.**
● Aber du arbeitest in Manchester, nicht wahr?
◆ **Ja, ich pendle.**
● Um wieviel Uhr stehst du normalerweise auf?
◆ **Normalerweise wache ich um sieben Uhr auf und stehe um zehn nach sieben auf.**
● Und um wieviel Uhr verlässt du das Haus?
◆ **Ich verlasse das Haus um halb acht.**

2 ● Sandra, um wieviel Uhr steht Michael auf?
◆ **Er steht um zehn nach sieben auf.**
● Wo arbeitet er?
◆ **Er arbeitet in Manchester und verlässt das Haus um halb acht.**
● Sandra, gehst du ins Fitnessstudio?
◆ **Ja, ich gehe manchmal ins Fitnessstudio.**
● Esst ihr zusammen zu Abend?
◆ **Ja, wir essen zusammen zu Abend.**
● Um wieviel Uhr esst ihr zu Abend?
◆ **Normalerweise essen wir um sieben Uhr zu Abend.**
● Und um wieviel Uhr entspannt ihr euch?
◆ **Wir entspannen uns um zehn Uhr. Normalerweise sehen wir zusammen fern.**

Page 22 Quiz

1 15.40; 2 früh; 3 climate change;
4 zweiundsiebzig; 5 mich; 6 Wir
verlasssen das Haus um halb sechs
und (wir) kommen um sieben Uhr an;
7 pendelt; 8 bad news – it means I am
sorry

Noch mehr 1

Pages 23–26

1 *a* 1 Ich wohne seit fast drei
   Monaten hier in München in der
   Nymphenburger Straße; 2 Seit
   fast drei Monaten wohne
   ich hier in München in der
   Nymphenburger Straße.

 b 1 Meine Schwester und ihr Mann
   wohnen seit 2010 in Mannheim; 2
   Seit 2010 wohnen meine Schwester
   und ihr Mann in Mannheim.

 c 1 Stefan studiert seit zwei Jahren an
   der Heidelberger Universität; 2 Seit
   zwei Jahren studiert
   Stefan an der Heidelberger
   Universität.

 d 1 Er ist seit vier Monaten mit Sylvia
   verheiratet; 2 Seit vier Monaten ist
   er mit Sylvia verheiratet.

 e 1 Ich bin seit acht Jahren mit
   Elisabeth verheiratet; 2 Seit acht
   Jahren bin ich mit Elisabeth
   verheiratet.

 f 1 Ich pendle seit zwei Monaten
   jeden Tag nach Augsburg; 2 Seit
   zwei Monaten pendle ich jeden Tag
   nach Augsburg.

2 *b* Um halb sechs steht er auf.
 c Um Viertel vor sechs duscht er sich.
 d Um sechs Uhr zieht er sich an.
 e Um sieben Uhr verlässt er das Haus.
 f Von acht Uhr bis siebzehn Uhr
   arbeitet er.
 g Um neunzehn Uhr kommt er nach
   Hause.
 h Von zwanzig bis dreiundzwanzig
   Uhr entspannt er sich.

3 In Großbritannien öffnen die
 Banken um neun Uhr morgens und
 schließen um vier Uhr nachmittags; In

Großbritannien öffnen die Geschäfte
um neun Uhr morgens und schließen
um halb sechs abends.

4 *a* Mein Bruder wohnt in Deutschland,
   weil er bei Lufthansa arbeitet.
 b Ich lerne Deutsch, weil ich
   Deutschland mag.
 c Sie spricht Englisch, weil sie in
   England wohnt.
 d Sie lernen Deutsch, weil sie in
   Österreich arbeiten möchten.
 e Er steht früh auf, weil die Arbeit um
   sieben Uhr morgens beginnt.

5 *a* Ich reise gern; *b* Ich trainiere gern
 im Fitnessstudio; *c* Ich pendle gern;
 d Ich lerne gern Deutsch; *e* Ich sehe
 gern fern.

6 *a* Schwager; *b* Schwiegermutter;
 c Enkel; *d* fünf; *e* Josef; *f* Robert;
 g drei; *h* Schwestern

7 *a* Ich heiße Ricardo Silva; ich bin
   Portugiese. Ich arbeite in Lisbon,
   bin Wissenschaftler und arbeite seit
   2001 bei Greenpeace. Ich spreche
   Portugiesisch, Deutsch und Englisch.
 b Ich wohne in Cascais in Portugal
   und pendle. Ich bin seit zwei Jahren
   verheiratet und habe zwei Kinder.
   Ich reise sehr gern und möchte in
   Brasilien arbeiten.

Unit 3

Page 28

2 ● Hallo, Lukas. Sag mal, was
   machst du normalerweise am
   Wochenende?
 ◆ Ich gehe ins Schwimmbad – ich
   schwimme besonders gern. Und ich
   spiele auch Fußball. Ich interessiere
   mich sehr für Fußball. Ich bin
   Bayern München Fan.
 ● Und du, Silke? Was machst du
   gerne? Interessierst du dich für
   Sport?
 ◆ Ich interessiere mich für
   Wassersport. Ich bin gerne am
   Meer. Am liebsten windsurfe ich.
 ● Elke, interessierst du dich für
   Wassersport?

◆ Nein, überhaupt nicht. Ich mache lieber Kung Fu – mir gefällt Kampfsport – mir gefallen alle Kampfsportarten! Ich gehe auch gern mit meiner Familie wandern.
Lukas: swimming; football (supports Bayern Munich); Silke: water sports, windsurfing; Elke: kung fu, martial arts, rambling.

3 ● Wir interessieren uns für die Natur und gehen gern wandern. Wir gehen oft in den Bergen oder in einem Nationalpark wandern. Uns gefallen lange Spaziergänge. Wir entdecken gerne idyllische Dörfer, bewundern gern das Panorama und genießen die Stille. Wir interessieren uns auch für die Flora und Fauna.

Page 29

6 **der Restaurantführer** *restaurant guide*; **der Hotelführer** *hotel guide*; **der Gastronomie- und Weinführer** *food and wine guide*; **die Liste der Führungen** *list of guided tours*; **der Veranstaltungs- und Messekalender** *calendar of events and trade shows*; **die Karte der Region** *map of the region*; **der Stadtplan** *town map*; **die Liste der Museumsöffnungszeiten** *list of museum opening times*; **der Sport- und Erlebnisführer** *sport and adventure guide*; **die Liste der Campingplätze** *list of campsites*

7 ● Guten Tag. Kann ich Ihnen helfen?
◆ Wann öffnet das Museum?
● Ich habe hier eine **Liste der Museumsöffnungszeiten**. Bitte schön.

◆ Haben Sie einen **Stadtplan**?
● Ja ... bitte ... Wir haben auch eine **Karte der Region**.

◆ Kann ich bitte diesen **Sport- und Erlebnisführer** kaufen?
● Gerne, aber er ist gratis. Ich habe auch eine interessante **Broschüre** hier.

◆ Wann sind die Stadtführungen?
● Wir haben hier eine **Liste der Führungen** – die nächste ist um elf Uhr.

◆ Gibt es hier in der Nähe ein gutes Restaurant?
● Ja, es gibt viele. Ich habe hier einen **Gastronomie- und Weinführer**. Das Restaurant Steinhofer ist sehr gut. Es ist hier in der Nähe.

◆ Muss man reservieren?
● Ja, das ist besser. Wenn Sie möchten, kann ich das Restaurant für Sie anrufen.

Page 30

2 & 3
● Was **kann** man hier in der Gegend machen?
◆ Also, wenn Sie gerne wandern, **können** Sie eine Naturlehrwanderung im Nationalpark machen. Wenn Sie lieber die Gegend mit dem Auto – oder mit dem Fahrrad – erkunden, gibt es hier viel zu **sehen**. Es gibt hier das Vogelschutzgebiet oder Sie können auch zum Weingut **gehen**. Oder wenn Sie sich für Kultur und Tradition **interessieren**, gibt es das Wieslocher Winzerfest. Das sollten Sie nicht **verpassen**!
Das Schloss is not mentioned.

Page 31

5 ● Ich interessiere mich für die Führung durch das Naturschutzgebiet. Kann man hier die Führung buchen?
◆ Ja, man kann hier im voraus buchen. Die Führung geht jeden Tag um neun Uhr von hier. Sie dauert vier Stunden.
● Muss man einen Pullover tragen?
◆ Ja, man sollte einen Pullover oder ein leichtes Sweatshirt mitbringen. Man muss feste Schuhe tragen, wie zum Beispiel Wanderschuhe, weil es im Naturschutzgebiet keine Wege gibt.

- Darf man im Naturschutzgebiet fotografieren?
- ◆ Ja, das darf man.
- Gut – kann man mit Kreditkarte bezahlen?
- ◆ Ja, natürlich!

Not mentioned: You need to bring food and water.

6 ● Hallo?
- ◆ Guten Tag. Ich möchte zwei Fahrräder mieten.
- Für wann?
- ◆ Für morgen früh, **von neun bis zwölf Uhr**.
- Ja, gerne.
- ◆ Was kostet das?
- **Ein Fahrrad kostet fünf Euro pro Stunde** oder fünfzehn Euro pro Tag.
- ◆ Gibt es eine Ermäßigung?
- **Nein, nicht für zwei Fahrräder, tut mir leid.** Es gibt eine Ermäßigung für Gruppen mit mindestens fünf Fahrrädern.
- ◆ Kann ich mit Kreditkarte bezahlen?
- Aber ja, sicher. Aber bringen Sie bitte Ihren Pass oder Ausweis.

3 hours; 5 euros per hour; none: discounts only available for 5 bikes minimum.

Page 32 Put it all together

1 *a* 4; *b* 2; *c* 5; *d* 7; *e* 3; *f* 1; *g* 6

2 *a* dich; *b* mir; *c* mich; *d* Ihnen

3 I don't have many hobbies. I like to go out with friends. I also like to go to town with my friends and do some shopping. We particularly like to go to the sports centre, where we play badminton and handball. I like playing badminton, but I prefer table tennis. You can also play squash there, but I am not very good at squash. I like tennis best – in summer I play with my sister every day.
I am also interested in photography. I often take photos – I like taking photos of nature best.

I like music because my aunt is a singer. And I like dancing – I go to dance lessons every Wednesday. What do you like doing in your spare time? Are you interested in photography too?

Page 33 Now you're talking!

1 ● Guten Tag. Kann ich Ihnen helfen?
- ◆ **Guten Tag. Haben Sie einen Gastronomie- und Weinführer?**
- Ja, bitte. Hier finden Sie alle Restaurants und Gaststätten.
- ◆ **Gibt es hier in der Nähe ein Restaurant?**
- Wenn Sie gerne deutsche Küche essen, gibt es das Haus Meier. Es hat einen guten Ruf.
- ◆ **Was kann man in Bremen machen?**
- Also, es gibt hier viel zu sehen und zu machen. Ich gebe Ihnen diesen Stadtführer und diesen Veranstaltungskalender.
- ◆ **Wir interessieren uns für die Natur. Können wir eine Führung im Nationalpark machen?**
- Im Nationalpark Harz gibt es Führungen zu Fuß, zu Pferd oder mit dem Mountainbike. Hier
- ◆ sind ein paar Informationen. Sie können im voraus buchen .... Sie müssen auch feste Schuhe tragen!
- **Kann ich hier in der Nähe ein Fahrrad mieten?**
- ◆ Ja, in der Steilstraße ... Hier ist ein Stadtplan .... die Steilstraße ist hier.

2 ● **Was machst du am Wochenende?**
- ◆ Also, ich gehe einkaufen, gehe mit meinen Freuden aus – wir gehen ins Kino, in die Disko ... und wir gehen zusammen essen.
- **Interessierst du dich für Sport?**
- ◆ Ja, ich interessiere mich für Sport. Ich spiele gern Volleyball. Mir gefällt auch Tischtennis.
- **Interessierst du dich für Fußball?**
- ◆ Fußball? Aber natürlich – ich bin Schalke 04-Fan. Aber sag mal, was machst du in deiner Freizeit?

3 He goes shopping, he goes out with friends, to the cinema and disco; they eat out together.

Page 34 Quiz

1 map of the region; 2 kann; 3 interessieren Sie sich; 4 your passport or ID; 5 they are all er/sie/es/man verb forms; 6 Ermäßigung – discount/ reduction, the others are all found in a tourist office; 7 The first sentence means Must we pay by credit card? and the second May we pay by credit card?; 8 not to be missed!

Unit 4

Page 36 & 37

2 *a* ● Ich suche ein weißes Hemd aus Leinen.
  ◆ Welche Größe?
  ● Achtundvierzig.

b ◆ Ich suche eine Jeans. Größe achtunddreißig.

c ● Bitte schön?
  ◆ Ich möchte ein schwarzes Top.
  ● Aus Baumwolle? Wolle? Seide?
  ◆ Aus Seide

d ● Ich suche eine graue Hose.
  ◆ Welche Größe?
  ● Sechsundvierzig.

e ◆ Ich suche einen grünen Pullover, aus Wolle oder Kaschmir. Größe M, vierzig oder zweiundvierzig.

f ● Kann ich Ihnen helfen?
  ◆ Nein, danke. Ich sehe mich nur um.

a white linen shirt, size 48; b pair of jeans, size 38; c black silk top; d grey trousers, size 46; e green jumper in pure wool or cashmere, size medium, 40 or 42; f buys nothing, just looking

3 ● Kann ich Ihnen helfen?
  ◆ Wir suchen ein blaues Kleid aus Baumwolle ... oder einen dunkelblauen Rock und eine hellblaue Bluse.
  ● Ja, gerne. Welche Größe haben Sie?
  ◆ Größe vierunddreißig, bitte – es ist für unsere Tochter.

● Mal sehen. Also, hier haben wir ein hellblaues Kleid aus Baumwolle. Und dann haben wir auch einen schönen Rock aus Wolle und eine sehr elegante Bluse aus Seide. Das hellblaue Kleid kostet achtundneunzig Euro, der dunkelblaue Rock kostet fünfundsiebzig Euro und die hellblaue Bluse kostet fünfzig Euro.
● Wir nehmen den dunkelblauen Rock und die hellblaue Bluse, bitte.
a cotton dress or a skirt and blouse; b dress: blue, skirt: navy, blouse: light blue; c their daughter; d skirt and blouse

5 ● Ich möchte diese Stiefel anprobieren.
  ◆ Welche Größe haben Sie?
  ● Achtunddreißig.
  ◆ Tut mir leid, aber wir haben sie nur in neunundreißig oder einundvierzig. Oder möchten Sie sie in schwarz anprobieren?
  ● Nein, danke.
  a 38; b 39 or 41; c black

6 *a* leicht (lightweight), wasserfest (waterproof), waschbar (washable), komfortabel (comfortable), geräumig (spacious), vordere (front), verstärkt (reinforced)
b i) Reißverschluss; ii) Tasche; iii) Seitentaschen

7 ● Ich habe diesen Rucksack gekauft, aber ich möchte ihn umtauschen, weil der Reißverschluss defekt ist.
  ◆ Kann ich mal sehen?
  ● Ja, bitte. Es ist dieser Reißverschluss hier, für das Seitenfach.
  a the zip's broken; b Ich möchte ihn umtauschen.

Page 38 & 39

2/3
  D Mutti, was hältst du von **dieser** Jacke? Steht sie mir?
  G Ich glaube, sie ist ein bisschen groß. Die Ärmel sind zu lang.
  S Sie gefällt mir nicht. Ich glaube, **diese** hier steht dir besser.

D Ach nein, Susanne! **Diese** da ist zu bunt. Mutti, **diese** Hose hier – ist sie zu lang? Sie ist nicht zu kurz, oder?

G Nein, sie ist perfekt. Und dazu **diese** schwarzen Schuhe. Was hältst du von **dieser** Krawatte?

D Na ja, **diese** da ist etwas blass ...

S Mir gefällt **diese** Fliege. Mit einem schönen, weißen Hemd und einer kanariengelben Weste.

a dieser; b diese; c diese, diese; d diese, dieser; e diese; f diese

5 The red one's more practical, more comfortable, more expensive; the yellow one's a bit tight, longer and it is not as expensive as the red one.

6 ● Dieses Kleid ist sehr **elegant**. Es ist modisch und die Farbe ist **sehr schön**.
◆ Mutti, dieses Kleid steht dir nicht. Es ist **total altmodisch** und die Farbe ist **scheußlich** *dreadful*!

Page 40 Put it all together

1 *a* weiß; *b* lang; *c* bunt; *d* groß; *e* modisch; *f* praktisch; *g* teuer

2 *a* weiße; *b* bunt; *c* schwarzen; *d* groß; *e* langärmeligen; *f* geräumig

3 *a* sie; *b* es; *c* ihn; *d* sie; *e* sie; *f* sie

4 *a* Ich suche eine Jeans in Größe achtunddreißig; *b* Ich suche ein weißes Hemd aus Leinen; *c* Ich suche eine dunkelblaue Jacke aus reiner Wolle, in Größe vierzig; *d* Ich suche einen leichten, wasserfesten Rucksack.

Page 41 Now you're talking!

1 ● Kann ich Ihnen helfen?
◆ Ich suche eine Jacke.
● Welche Größe haben Sie?
◆ Größe sechsundvierzig.
● Also. Wir haben Jacken aus Baumwolle, Leinen, Jeans ... oder möchten Sie vielleicht eine Jacke aus Wolle?
◆ Ja, ich möchte eine Jacke aus Wolle.
● Welche Farbe?
◆ Schwarz oder dunkelblau.

● Wir haben diese in dunkelblau aus reiner Wolle oder diese hier aus Wolle mit 40% Kaschmir.
◆ Kann ich die schwarze anprobieren?
● Ja, bitte – diese hier ist sehr schön.
◆ Was kostet sie?
● Sie ist sehr billig – nur €390!

2 ● Gibt es ein Problem?
◆ Ja, diese Brieftasche ist defekt, und ich möchte sie umtauschen.
● Kann ich mal sehen? Wo ist sie defekt?
◆ Hier, bitte.
● Leider haben wir keine anderen in dieser Art. Gefällt Ihnen diese hier?
◆ Was hältst du von dieser?
● Ich glaube, sie ist ein bisschen klein.

3 ● Gefallen dir diese? Stehen Sie mir?
◆ Ich glaube, sie sind ein bisschen eng.
● Aber sie sind so schön ... und sie sind im Angebot.
◆ Mir gefallen diese hier besser, und sie sind billiger.
● Toll! Sie sind fantastisch!

Page 42 Quiz

1 Ich sehe mich nur um; 2 Ich suche ...; 3 Are they too tight? 4 sun yellow; 5 Mir gefällt die graue (Jacke); 6 als; 7 Ich möchte diese hier anprobieren; 8 der Reißverschluss.

Noch mehr! 2

pages 43–46

1 *1 c* (Schleswig-Holstein); *2 d* (Brandenburg); *3 a* (Nordrhein-Westfalen); *4 b* (Bayern)

2 *a R; b F; c R; d F; e R; f F*

3 Liebe Heidemarie,
ich bin seit fünf Tagen in Bayern. Mir gefällt Bayern, weil man hier viel machen kann. Es gibt ein großes Schloss in der Nähe. Morgen miete ich ein Auto und erkunde die Dörfer. Heute Abend gibt es ein Winzerfest.

Das ist sehr interessant, weil ich mich für Wein interessiere.

4 *b* Muss ich jeden Tag trainieren?
 c Dürfen wir fernsehen?
 d Können wir die Gegend erkunden?
 e Müssen wir früh aufstehen?
 f Darf man sich am Abend entspannen?

5 *a* eine große; *b* ein kleines; *c* einen braunen; *d* eine rote; *e* eine schöne; *f* eine dunkelblaue; *g* ein gutes

6 *a* 4 Taschenlampen; *b* 4 Handtücher; *c* 4 Hüte; *d* 4 Jacken; *e* 4 Sonnenbrillen; *f* 4 Hosen; *g* 4 Ferngläser

Unit 5

Page 48

1 *a* Einfamilienhaus, Wohnung, Mietshaus, Reihenhaus, Landhaus; *b* Badezimmer, Abstellraum, Schlafzimmer, Keller, Küche, Diele, Esszimmer, Wohnzimmer, Toilette; *c* Garage, Garten, Terrasse; *d* zentral, hügelig, abgelegen, sonnig, historisch, ruhig.

Page 49

2 *a* ● Entschuldigen Sie bitte, können Sie mir bitte Ihr Haus oder Ihre Wohnung beschreiben?
 ◆ Ich wohne in einer **Neubau-Wohnung.** Sie ist klein, aber sehr **zentral gelegen** und sehr **gemütlich.** Meine Wohnung hat auch einen Balkon. Mein Balkon gefällt mir sehr gut.

 b ● Könnt ihr mir euer Haus beschreiben?
 ◆ Wir wohnen in einem **Landhaus,** circa 20 Kilometer von hier. Es ist total **renoviert.** Unser Haus befindet sich **in ruhiger Lage.**

 c ● Kannst du mir dein Haus oder deine Wohnung beschreiben?
 ◆ Ich wohne bei Freunden. Sie haben ein **Reihenhaus.** Es ist **modern,** es hat keinen Garten und die Terrasse ist sehr klein. Aber das Haus befindet sich nur

drei Kilometer von der Stadtmitte, was sehr **günstig gelegen** für die Arbeit ist.

3 ● Wie ist euer Haus?
 ◆ Wir haben eine große Küche, wo wir essen – wir haben kein Esszimmer – und ein Wohnzimmer. Wir haben drei Schlafzimmer, zwei Badezimmer und eine Toilette.
 ● Und draußen? Habt ihr eine Garage?
 ◆ Nein, wir haben keine Garage. Draußen ist ein sehr schöner Garten mit Bäumen, Blumen und mit Blick auf den Nationalpark – die Aussicht von unserer Terrasse ist ausgezeichnet.
 3 bedrooms; 2 bathrooms; no garage; superb view of National Park.

Page 50

1 *a* 3 bedrooms, 2 bathrooms; *b* 10 minutes; *c* yes; *d* trips to coast and harbour; *e* 1 050 euros.

3 ● Meier.
 ◆ Guten Tag. Mein Name ist Anna Kiel. Ich rufe aus England an. Ich beabsichtige, im August ein Ferienhaus in Norddeutschland zu mieten. Können Sie mir bitte ein paar Informationen über Ihr Haus geben?
 ● Ja, natürlich.
 ◆ Wie viele Schlafzimmer hat das Haus?
 ● Es gibt drei Schlafzimmer, insgesamt acht Schlafplätze. Es gibt eine Schlafcouch im Wohnzimmer.
 ◆ Und wie viele Badezimmer?
 ● Es gibt ein Badezimmer und eine Toilette im Erdgeschoss.
 ◆ Gibt es einen Garten?
 ● Es gibt einen Garten hinter dem Haus und auch eine Terrasse.
 ◆ Kann man parken?
 ● Ja, es gibt eine Garage.
 ◆ Gibt es eine Spülmaschine?
 ● Ja, ja, die Küche ist modern und komplett ausgestattet.

- Ist das Ferienhaus in der Nähe vom Meer?
- Der Strand ist zwei Kilometer entfernt, und es gibt auch ein öffentliches Schwimmbad.
- Was kostet das Haus pro Woche?
- Eintausendeinhundert Euro.

a 3; b yes, behind the house; c yes, there's a garage; d yes; e beach is 2 km away; f 1 100 euros.

Page 51

2
- Also, hier ist das Wohnzimmer.
- Was für ein schönes Zimmer! Und **so** groß und was für eine Aussicht!
- Hier haben wir die Küche – sie ist **sehr** geräumig. Der Ofen, die Spülmaschine und der Kühlschrank sind neu.
- Gibt es keine Waschmaschine?
- Ja, doch, aber sie ist im Keller. Hier sind die Gästeschlafzimmer. Das Schlafzimmer rechts hat ein Doppelbett, und das Schlafzimmer links hat ein Etagenbett.
- Es ist ein **bisschen** klein.
- Es ist **ziemlich** kompakt, das stimmt. Hier haben wir das Elternschlafzimmer. Und vergessen Sie nicht, dass das Wohnzimmer eine Schlafcouch hat. Also, machen Sie es sich gemütlich! Guten Aufenthalt!

3
a Zweifamilienhaus mit Garage: dreihunderttausend Euro
b herrliche Neubau-Wohnung: vierhundertfünfzigtausend Euro
c perfekt renoviertes Landhaus: achthundertzwanzigtausend Euro
d Einfamilienhaus, fünf Zimmer: vierhunderttausend Euro
e Landhaus mit fantastischer Aussicht: neunhundertfünfzigtausend Euro

a 300 000; b 450 000; c 820 000; d 400 000; e 950 000

Page 52 Put it all together

1 Küste/Berge; zentral/abgelegen; kompakt/geräumig; groß/klein; neu/alt; Land/Stadt. **Keller** *cellar* is left

2
a Diele; b Wohnzimmer; c Küche; d Esszimmer; e Badezimmer; f Schlafzimmer; g Terrasse; h Garage

3
a ZU VERMIETEN – Neubau-Einfamilienhaus, mit Blick aufs Meer, fünf Minuten vom Meer entfernt. Garten + sonnige Terrasse. drei Schlafzimmer; zwei Badezimmer
b ZU VERKAUFEN – Geräumiges Landhaus mit Panoramablick, ruhig, aber nicht abgelegen. Erdgeschoss: Diele, Wohnzimmer, ausgestattete Küche, Abstellraum. Erste Etage: vier Schlafzimmer, Badezimmer. Großer Garten, Garage.

Page 53 Now you're talking!

1
- Haus Ostsee, guten Morgen.
- **Ich beabsichtige, ein Haus in Norddeutschland zu mieten. Können Sie mir bitte das Haus Ostsee beschreiben?**
- Es ist ein schönes Reihenhaus mit Garten und Terrasse.
- **Ist es in der Nähe vom Meer?**
- Es befindet sich drei oder vier Kilometer von einem herrlichen Strand.
- **Was kostet es pro Woche?**
- Eintausendfünfhundert Euro.
- **Wie viele Schlafzimmer hat das Haus?**
- Das Haus hat drei Schlafzimmer. Es ist aber möglich, bis zu neun Personen zu beherbergen.
- **Und wie viele Badezimmer gibt es?**
- Es gibt ein großes Badezimmer auf der ersten Etage.
- **Gibt es eine Waschmaschine?**
- Ja, aber sicher.
- **Gibt es auch eine Spülmaschine?**
- Nein, eine Spülmaschine gibt es nicht.
- **Also, danke und auf Wiederhören.**

2
- Wie ist Ihr Haus?
- **Es ist ein Landhaus.**
- Wo befindet es sich?
- **Es befindet sich zehn Kilometer von Timmendorf.**

- Ist es ein großes Haus? Wie viele Zimmer hat das Haus?
- ◆ **Das Haus hat sechs Zimmer.**
- Sechs! Und wie viele Badezimmer?
- ◆ **Es gibt drei Badezimmer.**
- Prima! Haben Sie einen Garten?
- ◆ **Es gibt einen kleinen Garten und eine schöne Terrasse.**
- Also – auf Wiedersehen und guten Aufenthalt.

Page 54 Quiz

1 block of flats; 2 needs renovation; 3 eine Garage or ein Stellplatz; 4 dirty dishes; 5 Ihr; 6 Was für ein schönes Zimmer!; 7 ziemlich; 8 hügelig

Unit 6

Page 56 & 57

2 ● Entschuldigen Sie bitte, können Sie uns helfen? Wo befindet sich das Polizeirevier?
 ◆ Das Polizeirevier … es ist in der Bahnhofstraße. Sind Sie zu Fuß?
 ● Ja.
 ◆ Mal sehen … gehen Sie die Straße runter bis zur Ampel, gehen Sie rechts – nein, links – in die Rathausstraße. Gehen Sie immer geradeaus in Richtung Bahnhof. Sie sehen das Rathaus auf der linken Seite, gehen Sie am Rathaus rechts und dann müssen Sie die erste, nein, zweite … ach nein, die dritte Straße links nehmen. Gehen Sie die Straße entlang, überqueren Sie den Platz und Sie finden das Polizeirevier dort am Ende. Haben Sie verstanden?

3 ● Wir müssen bis zur Ampel gehen, dann links. Dann müssen wir immer geradeaus bis zum Rathaus gehen. Dort müssen wir nach links gehen und dann die dritte Straße links nehmen. Dann überqueren wir den Platz und das Polizeirevier befindet sich dort am Ende.
 It should be a right turn (not left) at the town hall.

4 ● Entschuldigen Sie bitte, wo gibt es hier in der Nähe einen Geldautomaten?
 ◆ Gehen Sie an der Ampel links und dann immer geradeaus. Gehen Sie dann sofort nach dem Rathaus links in Richtung Dom. Die Deutsche Bank ist hinter dem Dom, auf der rechten Seite und hat einen Geldautomaten draußen bei der Eingangstür.
 Turn left by the traffic lights, then go straight on. Go left immediately after the town hall, in the direction of the cathedral. Deutsche Bank is behind the cathedral, on the right-hand side, and the cash machine is outside by the entrance.

6 ● Entschuldigen Sie bitte, geht diese Straße zum Polizeirevier?
 ◆ Nein, Sie sind auf der falschen Straße. Das Polizeirevier ist in der Schäferstraße – ziemlich weit von hier. Aber Sie können den Bus nehmen, den Neunundsechziger – die Haltestelle ist ganz in der Nähe. Sie müssen am Bahnhof aussteigen. Gehen Sie dann die Meisterstraße entlang. Das Polizeirevier befindet sich nach zweihundert Metern auf der rechten Seite. Haben Sie verstanden?
 a quite far, in Schäferstraße; b 69; c very close; d the station; e Meisterstraße; f on the right after 200 metres.

Page 58

2 ● Hallo Stefanie. Hier ist Leo.
 ◆ Hallo, Leo, wie geht's?
 ● Hör mal, Stefanie, ich **habe** meinen Laptop **verloren.**
 ◆ Wie? Was **hast du gemacht**?
 ● Ich **habe gesagt**: Ich **habe** meinen Laptop **verloren**!
 ◆ Hast du eine Anzeige gemacht?
 ● Nein, noch nicht. Aber das **mache** ich sofort!
 ◆ Gut, dann viel Glück! Bis bald!

3 ● Hör mal, Frank. Wir verspäten uns ein bisschen. Wir haben den Laptop verloren.
◆ *Wir* haben ????
● Äh, also, *ich* habe den Laptop verloren.
Because Leo lost the laptop, but he's now saying 'we' lost it.

Page 59

2 suchen *to look for*; stecken *to put*; stellen *to place, stand*

3 ● Guten Tag, Herr Brand, guten Tag, Frau Brand. Also, was kann ich für Sie tun?
◆ Wir haben unseren Laptop verloren! Heute habe ich Briefmarken in der Post gekauft. Ich habe meinen Laptop auf den Boden gestellt und …
● Frau Brand, haben Sie den Laptop gesehen?
◆ Ja, ich habe ihn gesehen.
● … ich habe bezahlt. Dann habe ich die Brieftasche und meine Brille in die Tasche gesteckt. Ja, und dann habe ich den Laptop gesucht, aber ich habe ihn nicht gesehen.
◆ Moment mal, bitte. Haben Sie jemanden in der Nähe gesehen?
● Nein, ich habe niemanden gesehen.
◆ Und Sie Frau Brand? Haben Sie etwas gesehen?
● Nein, ich habe nichts gesehen.
Order of events: d, a, e, c, b

4 Er hat Briefmarken gekauft; er hat den Laptop auf den Boden gestellt; er hat bezahlt; er hat die Brieftasche und die Brille in die Tasche gesteckt; er hat den Laptop gesucht; er hat ihn nicht gesehen.

5 *a* niemand *b* jemanden *c* jemand

Page 60 Put it all together

1 *a* Was hast du gesagt?
b Ich habe niemanden gesehen.
c Ich habe nichts gesehen.
d Ich habe das Polizeirevier angerufen.

e Ich habe nicht verstanden.
f Was haben Sie gemacht?

2 *a* verloren; *b* gesehen; *c* verstanden; *d* gegessen; *e* gestellt; *f* gekauft; *g* gesucht; *h* angerufen

3 *a* Ich habe **ihn** verloren.
b Habt ihr **es** gesehen?
c Wir haben **es** verstanden.
d Er hat **es** gegessen.
e Leo hat **ihn** auf den Boden gestellt.
f Hast du **ihn** gekauft?
g Ich habe **sie** gesucht.
h Er hat **sie** angerufen

Page 61 Now you're talking!

1 ● **Entschuldigen Sie bitte, können Sie uns bitte helfen?**
◆ Ja, was kann ich für Sie tun?
● **Wo befindet sich das Polizeirevier?**
◆ In der Weststraße.
● **Entschuldigen Sie bitte. Geht diese Straße zum Polizeirevier?**
◆ Ja, es ist nicht weit. Gehen Sie die Straße runter bis zur Ampel. Dort gehen Sie links. Gehen Sie dann die Straße entlang bis zur Marktstraße, dann rechts und Sie finden die Weststraße auf der linken Seite. Das Polizeirevier ist am Ende der Straße, auf der rechten Seite. Haben Sie verstanden?
● **Ja, ich habe verstanden. Danke.**

2 It's not far. Down here to the lights, turn left, go along the road as far as Marktstraße, turn right and Weststraße is on the left. The police station is at the end of the road, on the right-hand side.

3 ● Paul Hölzner.
◆ **Hallo Paul. Gibt es ein Problem?**
● Ja, Stefan hat …
◆ **Was hast du gesagt?**
● Stefan hat sein Handy verloren. Hast du es gesehen?
◆ **Ja, ich habe es gestern bei Frauke gesehen.**

- Er hat alles verloren – Daten, Termine, Telefonnummern. Er ist total gestresst.
- **Hat er Frauke angerufen?**
- Nein, noch nicht ... Und ihr zwei, was habt ihr heute gemacht?
- **Wir haben einen Ausflug nach Köln gemacht.**
- Und wo habt ihr gegessen?
- **Wir haben zu Mittag in einer Kneipe auf dem Rathausplatz gegessen.**
- Prima!

Page 62 Quiz

1 110, Polizeirevier; 2 very close; 3 if you have understood; 4 etwas; 5 falsche Nummer; 6 Geht diese Straße zum Bahnhof? 7 aussteigen; 8 ich habe gekauft, ich habe verkauft

Noch mehr 3

Pages 63–66

1

	1	2
within reach of Blausee Naturpark	✓	✓
quiet location	✓	✓
shops not too far	?	✓
somewhere to eat outside	?	✓
car parking	✓	✓
sleeps 4 comfortably	✓	✓
2 bathrooms	x	✓
large kitchen	✓	?
heating	?	✓

2 Dear Mr Waldbach
I intend to spend two weeks with my wife and two friends near Kandersteg and Blausee. Can you tell me if your house, Berghaus Kandersteg, is available from 22 September until 6 October? Can you tell me the weekly rate for this period, including the use of the garage? We would also like to know if there is a washing machine and if the kitchen area has a freezer.
Best wishes

3 Lieber Herr Waldbach,
ich beabsichtige, eine Woche mit meinen drei Freunden in der Nähe von Kandersteg und Blausee zu verbringen. Können Sie mir mitteilen, ob Ihr Haus, das Berghaus Kandersteg, vom 28. Juli bis 4. August frei ist? Können Sie mir auch sagen, wie hoch die Wochenrate für diese Zeitspanne ist, inklusive Versicherung? Ich möchte auch gerne erfahren, wie viele Schlafzimmer das Haus hat und ob es eine Spülmaschine gibt.
Mit freundlichen Grüßen

4 The cheese fondue tasted good.

5 gemacht – machen; gesehen – sehen; besucht – besuchen; fotografiert – fotografieren; entspannt – (sich) entspannen; ferngesehen – fernsehen; gefunden – finden; gegessen – essen; probiert – probieren; geschmeckt – schmecken; gekauft – kaufen

6 Liebe Sarah,
Gestern Nachmittag habe ich das Museum und das Schloss besucht. Im Dorf habe ich ein Buch gekauft.
Ich habe viel gesehen und habe viel fotografiert. Am Abend habe ich *Steak und Kidney Pie* probiert – es hat nicht gut geschmeckt!
Schreibe mir bald!
Hannelore

7 *1* Name: Welling/Wahrig; *2* geboren in Ratingen/Regensburg; *3* wohnhaft in Mayerhoferstraße 23/Hofstraße 26; *4* schwarze/braune Brieftasche; *5* Inhalt €200/€300; *6* Führerschein/Pass; *7* Gesamtwert €235/€350; *8* verloren am 5./6. März; *9* verloren am Nachmittag/Morgen; *10* verloren im Sportzentrum/Einkaufszentrum *11.* in Jackentasche gelassen/im Rucksack gelassen

Unit 7

Page 68

2 ● Wohin fährst du dieses Jahr auf Urlaub?
  ◆ Ich fahre mit meinen Freunden nach München.
  ● Und Sie, wohin fahren Sie diesen Sommer auf Urlaub?
  ◆ Auf die Insel Rügen, mit meiner Familie. Ich habe die Insel noch nie gesehen.
  ● Wohin fahrt ihr dieses Jahr auf Urlaub?
  ◆ Wir fahren in den Schwarzwald. Mein Bruder hat ein Landhaus 15 Kilometer von Freiburg.
  ● Ihr Glücklichen!
  ◆ Wohin fährst du dieses Jahr auf Urlaub?
  ● Ich fahre mit meiner Freundin ans Meer.
  ◆ Wohin fahren Sie dieses Jahr auf Urlaub?
  ● Diesen Sommer fahre ich zu meiner Tante. Sie wohnt in der Nähe von Bern.

3 ● Entschuldigen Sie bitte, wohin **fahren** Sie dieses Jahr auf Urlaub?
  ◆ Diesen Sommer hoffe ich, nach Lübeck zu **fahren** – alleine! Ich bin geschieden, und meine Tochter **fährt** mit meinem Ex-Mann auf Urlaub. Sie **fahren** in die Karibik – zur Oma.

Page 69

1 ● Wie ist das Wetter in Bad Mergentheim?
  ◆ Also ... im **Sommer**, im Juli und August, **ist das Wetter gut, es ist warm**, und auch in den Bergen, mit einer Temperatur im Durchschnitt von 23 Grad. Im Winter **schneit es oft** – wir fahren immer eine Woche auf Winterurlaub. Aber im Winter **ist es auch sonnig.**

Summer: good weather, warm; winter: often snows, sunny; average temperature is 23 degrees

Page 70 & 71

2 ● Hallo. Wohin bist du letztes Jahr auf Urlaub gefahren?
  ◆ Ich bin ans Meer gefahren.
  ● Wohin sind Sie letztes Jahr auf Urlaub gefahren?
  ◆ Ich bin wie jedes Jahr in die Alpen gefahren. Ich gehe gern wandern.
  ● Entschuldigung, wohin sind Sie letztes Jahr auf Urlaub gefahren?
  ◆ Ich bin nach Österreich gefahren, genauer gesagt nach Kufstein.
  ● Herr und Frau Meier, wohin sind Sie letztes Jahr auf Urlaub gefahren?
  ◆ Wir sind nach München gefahren. Es war sehr warm.
  ● Hallo. Sag mal, wohin bist du letztes Jahr auf Urlaub gefahren?
  ◆ Ich bin zu meiner Oma nach England gefahren. Ich bin zwei Wochen geblieben.
  ● Wohin sind Sie letztes Jahr auf Urlaub gefahren?
  ◆ Letztes Jahr sind wir nicht auf Urlaub gefahren. Unsere Freunde aus Frankreich sind nach Deutschland gekommen.

3 *a* Ich bin mit meiner Freundin nach Berlin gefahren.
  b Wir sind letztes Jahr mit dem Schiff in die Karibik gefahren.
  c Wir sind mit Freunden nach England gefahren.
  d Bist du gestern nach Aachen gefahren?

5 ● Hallo, Sebastian. Hattest du viel Spaß?
  ◆ Es war ausgezeichnet!
  ● Was hast du gemacht? Wohin bist du gefahren?
  ◆ Ich bin mit Birgit, meiner Freundin, an die Ostsee gefahren. Wir haben auch die Insel Rügen besucht. Warst du schon einmal auf Rügen?
  ● Nein, ich war noch nie dort.

He went to the Baltic sea and visited the island of Rügen with his girlfriend Birgit.

6 ● Was habt ihr gemacht?
◆ Am Donnerstag sind wir nach Rügen gefahren. Es war sehr schön. Wir sind mit der Fähre von Stralsund gefahren und sind gegen elf Uhr in Altefähr angekommen. Wir sind mit dem Bus nach Putbus gefahren. Wir haben ein kleines Restaurant gefunden und haben dort fabelhaften Fisch gegessen. Nach dem Mittagessen sind wir ein bisschen durch die Straßen gegangen. Dann haben wir die Kirche im Schlosspark gesehen. Um sechs Uhr sind wir wieder in den Bus gestiegen. Wir sind um neun Uhr abends nach Stralsund zurückgekehrt. Es war ausgezeichnet.

Correct order: j, b, f, d, i, a, g, e, c, h

Page 72 Put it all together

1 *a* 3; *b* 5; *c* 6; *d* 4; *e* 2; *f* 1.

2 *a* habt ... gegessen; *b* seid ... gefahren; *c* bin ... gekommen; *d* sind ... gestiegen; *e* ist ... geblieben; *f* hat ... fotografiert; *g* ist ... zurückgekehrt; *h* sind ... angekommen; *i* haben ... gefunden.

3 Vor zwei Jahren bin ich mit meinen Freunden auf die Insel Rügen auf Urlaub gefahren. Wir sind mit der Fähre von Stralsund gefahren und sind in Altefähr angekommen.

4 *a* Ich fahre alleine ans Meer.
b Wir fahren mit zwei Freunden nach Frankreich.
c Ich fahre mit meiner Familie nach Bayern.
d Wir fahren dieses Jahr nicht auf Urlaub; wir bleiben zuhause.

Page 73 Now you're talking

1 ● Sag mal, wie ist das Wetter heute?
◆ **Es ist schön und sonnig.**
● Ist es kalt?
◆ **Nein, es ist achtzehn Grad.**

2 *a* ● Wohin fährst du dieses Jahr auf Urlaub?

◆ Ich fahre ans Meer.
● Fährst du alleine?
◆ **Nein, ich fahre mit meinen Freunden.**

b ● Fahren Sie diesen Sommer nach Österreich?
◆ **Ja, ich hoffe, mit meiner Partner nach Kärnten zu fahren.**
● Eine schöne Region. Fahren Sie in die Berge?
◆ **Ja, meine Kusine hat ein Haus in der Nähe von Ratingen.**
● Sie Glücklichen! Ich war vor zwei Jahren dort.

3 ● Waren Sie schon einmal in Österreich?
◆ **Ich bin letztes Jahr nach Österreich gefahren. Ich bin mit Freunden gefahren.**
● Hatten Sie viel Spaß?
◆ **Es war ausgezeichnet!**
● Wie war das Wetter?
◆ **Es war sehr heiß – fünfunddreißig Grad!**

Page 74 Quiz

1 Vor drei Jahren; 2 Ich war noch nie in Deutschland; 3 fährst; 4 kommen, fahren; 5 bleiben (to stay) – it takes sein; 6 das Wetter ist schrecklich; 7 es ist heiß is present, es war heiß is past; 8 anrufen

Unit 8

Pages 76–77

2 Sonja's not going into work because she's not well.

3 ● Sonja, geht's dir nicht gut?
◆ Nein, mir geht's furchtbar.
● Was ist los?
◆ Ich **kann** nicht laufen. Aua! Astrid, **mir** geht's so schlecht.
● Du Arme! Aber **was** ist los? Gab **es** einen Unfall?
◆ Einen Unfall? Nein. Gestern **bin** ich mit Ludwig ausgegangen. Wir sind aufs Land **gefahren** und **sind** mindestens hundert Kilometer gewandert.

- Sonja, übertreibe nicht!
- Na ja, mindestens **zehn** Kilometer. Und ich **bin** gefallen.
- Sonja, ich habe **viel** zu tun. Tschüs!

4 Hans-Jörg, hallo. Sonja geht heute nicht zur Arbeit. Ihr geht es nicht gut, weil sie gestern mit Ludwig aufs Land gefahren und gefallen ist. Liebe Grüße

5 ● Geht's dir besser?
- Nein. Aua! Mein Rücken tut weh, mein Knie tut weh und meine Beine tun auch weh.
- Wenn dein Knie weh tut, musst du zum Arzt gehen.

Her back, knee and legs hurt.

6 ● Gabriele, ich bin's, Sonja.
- Sonja, hallo. Hör mal, ich kann heute nicht lange reden. Peter geht's nicht gut. Der Arme **hat Halsschmerzen, Kopfschmerzen, die Schultern tun ihm weh, und er hat Husten.** Aber wie geht es dir?

Page 78

2 ● Ich habe mein Knie verstaucht.
- Aha. Mal sehen ... Was ist passiert?
- Ich bin gefallen. Es tut weh.
- Können Sie es bewegen?
- Ein bisschen, aber es ist schwierig.
- Hm. Das Knie ist ein bisschen geprellt – aber nichts Ernstes. Nehmen Sie ein Schmerzmittel, ruhen Sie und bewegen Sie es nicht viel.
- Ist das alles?
- Ja, in zwei oder drei Tagen, wird alles in Ordnung sein.

3 ● Nehmen Sie zwei von diesen Kapseln mit Wasser, alle vier Stunden, am besten nach den Mahlzeiten. Es ist wichtig, keinen Alkohol zu trinken und nicht die Dosis zu überschreiten.

Take two capsules with water every four hours, preferably after meals. It's important not to drink any alcohol and not to exceed the recommended dose.

Page 79

1 Akkupunktur, ausgewogene Diät, Harmonie, holistische Medizin, Homöopathie, inneres Wohlbefinden, Massage, persönlicher Trainer, gestresst

Page 80 Put it all together

1 *a* Knöchel; *b* Trainer; *c* gestern; *d* Unfall

2 *a* 4; *b* 3; *c* 2; *d* 1; *e* 5

3 Hallo, Daniel. Tut mir leid, aber ich kann dich heute Abend nicht treffen. Mir geht's nicht gut, ich habe Fieber und meine Arme und Beine tun weh. Marion hat Halsschmerzen und Kopfschmerzen. Und wie geht's dir? Bist du heute zur Arbeit gegangen? Hast du Uwe gesehen? Tschüs

Page 81 Now you're talking!

1 ● **Hallo! Geht's dir gut?**
- Nein, mir geht's nicht gut. Mir geht's gar nicht gut.
- **Was ist los?**
- Mein Rücken tut weh und mein Knie tut weh.
- **Du Arme! Was ist passiert?**
- Was ist passiert? Gestern ist passiert!
- **Hattest du gestern viel Spaß?**
- Ludwig, gestern sind wir 20 Kilometer gewandert und heute kann ich nicht aufstehen. Ich kann nicht ...
- **Wir sind fünf Kilometer gewandert. Also ... ich habe viel zu tun.**

2 ● Wie geht es Ihnen heute?
- **Mir geht es nicht gut.**
- Das tut mir leid. Was ist los?
- **Ich habe Kopfschmerzen und Halsschmerzen.**
- Sie Arme(r)!
- **Und meine Schultern tun weh.**
- Haben Sie Fieber?
- **Ja, und ich habe Husten und Ohrenschmerzen.**

- Ich glaube, Sie haben Grippe. Haben Sie etwas eingenommen?
- **Nein, aber ich möchte ein Schmerzmittel.**
- Ich habe ein sehr wirksames homöopathisches Medikament. Einen Augenblick, bitte.

Page 82 Quiz

1 Notaufnahme, 112; 2 Ihr geht's besser; 3 mein Fuß tut weh, meine Füße tun weh; 4 acupuncture is Chinese, shiatsu massage is Japanese; 5 Sie hat Magenschmerzen; 6 Alkohol (all the others are types of medication) 7 Alles wird in Ordnung sein; 8 I can't chat for long today.

Noch mehr 4

Pages 83–86

1 *a* habe; *b* haben; *c* sind; *d* bin; *e* habe; *f* ist; *g* bin; *h* hat; *i* habe; *j* ist

2 *g, e, c, j, f, d, b, i, a, h*
Her name is Andrea Friedrichsen; she was born in Baden-Baden in 1928. Two years after the end of the Second World War she got married. In the 50s she and her husband went to Australia with their children. In 1981 her daughter moved to Vienna. Four years ago her husband died. Last year she returned to Germany. Six months ago her daughter and son-in-law bought a house in Leipzig. A fortnight ago she decided to look for her old classmates. Last week she wrote a letter to the local paper. Yesterday the postman brought two replies to her letter.

3 Kurort, Thermalquellen, gegründet, Kurtourismus, und genießen, Wasserbehandlung

4 *a* We come from the North of Germany. We come here to Baden-Baden mainly because my wife suffers from arthritis and the hot springs are very good for her. We will also go on a yoga course this year.

b We love hydrotherapy, but where we live there are unfortunately no hot springs. For this reason, we come to Baden-Baden every year. This year we will also take part in a diet programme.

c I have come here to have hydrotherapy. This year I will also do water aerobics.

d We come to Baden-Baden every year because we like the treatments. This year we will also hire bikes.

- Warum sind Sie nach Baden-Baden gekommen?
- Ich bin hierher gekommen, um Hydrotherapie und Unterwassermassagen zu bekommen. In diesem Jahr werde ich auch Wasseraerobic machen.
- Warum sind Sie hier in Baden-Baden?
- Wir kommen jedes Jahr nach Baden-Baden, weil wir die Behandlungen mögen. Dieses Jahr werden wir auch Fahrräder mieten.
- Woher kommen Sie und warum sind Sie hierher gekommen?
- Wir kommen aus Norddeutschland. Wir kommen hauptsächlich hierher nach Baden-Baden, weil meine Frau an Arthritis leidet und die Therme sehr gut für sie sind. Wir werden dieses Jahr auch einen Yoga-Kurs machen.
- Warum sind Sie hier?
- Wir lieben Wasserbehandlungen, aber wo wir wohnen, gibt es leider keine Thermalquellen. Wir kommen aus diesem Grund jedes Jahr nach Baden-Baden. Dieses Jahr werden wir auch an einem Diätprogramm teilnehmen.
- Warum sind Sie nach Baden-Baden gekommen?
- Als Kind bin ich jedes Jahr mit meinen Eltern auf Urlaub hierher gekommen. Meine Eltern haben diesen Kurort geliebt. Dieses Jahr

bin ich mit meinen Kindern hier, und wir werden das Stadtmuseum und das Schloss besuchen.

As a child, I used to come to the area on holiday with my parents. My parents loved this spa resort. This year I am in Baden-Baden with my children and we will visit the town museum and the castle.

5 *a* Letztes Jahr haben wir an einem Diätprogramm teilgenommen.
b Letztes Jahr haben wir Fahrräder gemietet.
c Letztes Jahr habe ich Wasseraerobic gemacht.

6 In den Sommermonaten **Juli** und **August** liegen die Temperaturen in Baden-Baden bei circa fünfundzwanzig Grad. Aber sowohl im Juni als auch im September erreichen die Temperaturen eine Höhe von über **zwanzig** Grad. Im Sommer liegen die Nachttemperaturen zwischen zehn und dreizehn Grad. August ist der **sonnigste** Monat und **September** ist der trockenste Monat. Im Winter liegen die Temperaturen zwischen null und **fünf** Grad, und **es schneit sehr oft**. Die **Nachttemperaturen** im Winter liegen oft **unter null** Grad.
a July, August; b 20°C; c summer, 13°C; d sunniest, September; e 0 and 5°C; f snow/ it snows very often; g night, below 0°C.

7 *a* Erkältungssirup, 3;
b Kopfschmerztabletten, 1;
c Nasenspray 4; *d* Magenpulver 6;
e Augentropfen 2; *f* Halspastillen 5

8 *a* She can't leave her son (17) on his own – he fell while playing football and broke his leg.
b A friend who would like to come instead.

9 Sehr geehrte Frau Petzold,
mein Name ist Mark Taylor und ich bin ein Freund von Frau Robertson. Sie hat ihre Reservierung storniert, weil ihr Sohn beim Fußballspiel gefallen ist und sein Bein gebrochen hat. Stattdessen möchte ich vom 21. bis 28. April zum Gasthof Zur Krone kommen.
Mit freundlichen Grüßen
M. Taylor

Unit 9

Page 88

1 *a* Feinschmecker; *b* im Freien; *c* zubereiten; *d* einladen

2 *a* 1 Boris, 2 Julia, 3 Gesine
b 8pm Friday on the terrace of the Forsthaus.

Page 89

4 • Hallo **Katharina**, hier ist Guido. Möchtest du am Freitagabend zum Abendessen ins Forsthaus kommen? Wir feiern Claudias Geburtstag.
♦ Was für eine nette Idee. Mit Vergnügen!

• **Jan,** guten Morgen. Hier ist Guido. An diesem Freitag ist Claudias Geburtstag, und wir haben ein Abendessen organisiert, um ihn zu feiern. Die Feier wird diesen Freitag Abend, um acht Uhr, auf der Terrasse des Forsthauses stattfinden. Möchten Sie auch kommen?
♦ **Ja, ich komme mit dem größten Vergnügen! Herzlichen Dank. Um wie viel Uhr?**

• Hallo **Nico**, hier ist Guido. Möchtet ihr, du und Liliane, zu einer Feier kommen? Wir haben am Freitag Abend ein Abendessen …
♦ Ah, Guido, **tut mir leid, aber am Freitag können wir nicht kommen. Wie schade!**

5 • Hier ist Fabian. Hallo Guido – danke für die Einladung. Es tut mir sehr leid, aber ich kann nicht zum Abendessen kommen, **weil ich am Freitag nach München fahre.** Grüße an Claudia. Tschüs.
Because he's going to Munich.

6 ● Hallo, meine Liebe. Hast du meine E-Mail erhalten?
◆ Ja, habe ich.
● Und? Hast du Lust, zu der Feier zu kommen?
◆ Tja ... **ich weiß nicht, ob ich kann.** Wo ist sie?
She doesn't know if she can come.

Pages 90–91

2 ● Kommt Gesine zum Abendessen?
◆ Ich **weiß** nicht.
● Warum **weißt** du es nicht?
◆ Ich habe gesagt, ich **weiß** nicht, ob sie kommen **kann**.
● Wie unfreundlich!

3 ● Kennst du Gesine?
◆ Ich kenne sie nicht gut.
● Sie kommt nicht zum Abendessen – Pascal ist sehr **enttäuscht**. Sie ist **gemein**.
◆ Pascal glaubt, sie ist **lieb** und **nett**.
● Ich glaube, sie ist total **unfreundlich**.
◆ Ich stimme dir zu. Und sie ist **unhöflich**.
● Armer Pascal. Er ist so **sympathisch** ... **höflich** und **gut**.
◆ Wie schade, dass er eine Schwäche für Gesine hat.
P: enttäuscht, höflich, sympathisch, gut; G: unhöflich, gemein, lieb, nett, unfreundlich
Yes, Guido agrees with Christine: Ich stimme dir zu.

5 ● Ich habe eine Nachricht von Gudrun erhalten.
◆ Wer ist Gudrun?
● Sie besucht den Fotografie-Kurs.
◆ Wie sieht sie aus? Ah ja, sie ist dunkelhaarig und schlank, nicht wahr?
● Nein, **sie ist blond, etwas mollig und ungefähr ein Meter fünfundsiebzig groß.**
◆ Nein, ich kenne sie nicht.
Gudrun is blonde, a bit chubby, 1.75m tall.

6 ● Ich kenne sie nicht.
◆ Doch, du kennst sie. **Braune Augen. Langes, glattes Haar.**
● Ah, Gudrun. Das Mädchen mit den langen Beinen? Die immer lächelt?
◆ Genau!
Her hair is long and straight; her eyes are brown.

7 ● Hat Boris geantwortet?
◆ Wer ist Boris? Der kleine, dicke Typ, mit einem Schnäuzer?
● Nein. **Er ist nicht dick. Er ist weder dick noch dünn. Normalerweise kleidet er sich sportlich, mit Jeans und Tennisschuhen. Er ist fast zwei Meter groß und atemberaubend gutaussehend.**
◆ Mmmmm?!
Neither fat nor thin, he usually dresses casually in jeans and trainers; he's nearly 2 metres tall and breathtakingly good-looking.

Page 92 Put it all together

1 *a* Lasst uns ins Restaurant gehen!
b Sollen wir im Freien essen?
c Lasst uns in die Diskothek gehen.
d Ich habe Lust auf die Kneipe.
e Sollen wir morgen nach Berlin fahren?
f Ich schlage vor, wir machen eine Weinprobe.
g Ich habe Lust auf das Theater.

2 klein *short*, groß *tall*; kurz *short*, lang *long*; höflich *polite*, unhöflich *rude*; dünn *thin*, dick *fat*; blond *blonde*, dunkelhaarig *dark*; unsympathisch *unpleasant*, sympathisch *pleasant*; schlank *slim*, mollig *chubby*; unfreundlich *unfriendly*, freundlich *friendly*

3 eingeladen, feiern, gehen, lasst

4 Lieber Tim,
du bist herzlich zu einer Feier am Freitag, den 12. Oktober eingeladen. Ich habe ein Abendessen um acht Uhr im Gasthof Meistertrunk organisiert,

um meinen Geburtstag zu feiern.
Bitte lass mich bis zum 30. September
wissen, ob du kommen kannst.
Liebe Grüße

5 a Danke für die Einladung. Was für
      eine nette Idee! Ich komme mit
      dem größten Vergnügen!
   b Tut mir leid. Wie schade! Ich kann
      nicht kommen, weil ich auf Urlaub
      fahre.

Page 93 Now you're talking!

1 ● Weißt du, dass Marlene nicht zur
     Konferenz geht?
   ◆ **Ich kenne Marlene nicht.**
   ● Doch, du kennst sie. Sie arbeitet mit
     Georg und Lavinia.
   ◆ **Wie sieht sie aus? Ist sie groß?**
   ● Also ... nein, sie ist weder groß noch
     klein. Zirka ein Meter siebzig. Sie hat
     lockiges Haar und braune Augen.
   ◆ **Ist sie blond? Schlank?**
   ● Blond, ja. Und ziemlich schlank.
   ◆ **Ach ja, ich kenne Marlene – sie ist
     sehr sympathisch.**
   ● Sympathisch? Marlene? Ich glaube,
     sie ist nicht sehr sympathisch.

2 ● Hallo. Wir haben uns schon lange
     nicht gesehen! Hör mal, ich möchte
     gerne mit dir ausgehen, um meinen
     Geburtstag zu feiern.
   ◆ **Was für eine gute Idee! Mit
     Vergnügen!**
   ● Also, ich habe geplant, wir gehen
     am Dienstag in die Diskothek in der
     Kirchhofstraße.
   ◆ **Tut mir leid, am Dienstag kann
     ich nicht, weil ich nach Tübingen
     fahre.**
   ● Oh je, wie schade! Aber hör
     mal, ich möchte zu Martas
     Geburtstagsfeier gehen. Sie wird am
     3. Dezember stattfinden. Möchtest
     du auch kommen?
   ◆ **Herzlichen Dank, ja, ich komme
     mit dem größten Vergnügen.
     Herzlichen Glückwunsch und
     Grüße an Marta.**

3 ● Wie sieht Leo aus?
   ◆ **Er ist atemberaubend
     gutaussehend: er ist dunkelhaarig,
     hat braune Augen, ist ein Meter
     achtzig groß und kleidet sich
     sportlich.**

Page 94 Quiz
*1 Schnäuzer (moustache); 2 accepted
– it means: with great pleasure; 3 eine
Weinprobe; 4 die Feier hat am Samstag
stattgefunden – past tense: the party
took place; die Feier wird am Samstag
stattfinden – future tense: the party
will take place 5 ich weiß sie nicht –
knowing a fact; 6 ich habe Lust*

Unit 10

Page 96

2 ● Es ist nicht schwierig, Knödel zu
     kochen, wenn Sie dem Rezept
     gut folgen. Schneiden Sie sechs
     alte Brötchen in Stückchen.
     Braten Sie eine gehackte Zwiebel
     und etwas Petersilie in Butter.
     Vermischen Sie dann alles mit den
     Brötchenstücken. Erwärmen Sie
     etwas Milch und gießen Sie sie
     über den Brötchenteig. Vermischen
     Sie drei Eier mit Pfeffer und Salz
     und gießen Sie sie über den Teig.
     Formen Sie mit nassen Händen
     tennisballgroße Knödel. Geben
     Sie die Knödel in heißes, aber
     nicht kochendes Wasser, weil die
     Knödel sonst auseinanderfallen.
     Das ist eine goldene Regel! Nach
     20 Minuten sind die Knödel fertig –
     Guten Appetit!
   d, a, b, h, e, c, f, g

3 The water must not boil, because the
   dumplings will fall apart otherwise.

Page 97

2 Vorspeise: Champignoncremesuppe;
   Hauptspeise: Schweinebraten mit
   gerösteten Frühkartoffeln und
   Rotkohl; Nachspeise: Apfelstrudel
   mit Sahne

3 ● Haben Sie passende Weine zu den Gängen?

◆ Ja, wir servieren unser Abendessen heute mit verschiedenen Weinen. Als Aperitif gibt es einen trockenen, eleganten Sekt, der ungefähr 10% Alkohol enthält.

● Wird der Sekt kalt serviert?

◆ Ja, sehr kalt, zwischen fünf und acht Grad.

● Und was wird zur Vorspeise getrunken?

◆ Für die Champignoncremesuppe haben wir einen Weißherbst, also einen leichten Roséwein, oder einen Gewürztraminer, also einen fruchtigen Weißwein.

● Werden diese Weine kalt oder auf Raumtemperatur serviert?

◆ Beide Weine werden kalt serviert.

● Und für die Hauptspeise?

◆ Für den Schweinebraten haben wir einen jungen Dornfelder, mit anderen Worten, einen Rotwein, aus dem Jahre 2010. Natürlich kann man nach Geschmack auch Bier oder Apfelwein trinken.

● Wie schmeckt der Dornfelder?

◆ Der Dornfelder ist halbtrocken und vollmundig. Und dann am Ende des Essens gibt es einen Apfelstrudel mit Sahne. Dazu servieren wir eine ausgereifte Trockenbeerenauslese, einen sehr lieblichen Wein.

Aperitif: Sekt; Vorspeise: Weißherbst or Gewürztraminer; Hauptspeise: Dornfelder or Bier or Apfelwein; Nachspeise: Trockenbeerenauslese

4 Sekt – trocken, elegant; Weißherbst – rosé, leicht; Gewürztraminer – weiß, fruchtig; Dornfelder – rot, jung, halbtrocken, vollmundig; Trockenbeerenauslese – ausgereift, lieblich

Page 98

2 ● Andreas, möchtest du diesen Weißwein probieren?

◆ Mm ... trocken, leicht, delikat ... er hat einen eleganten Geschmack.

● Dieser Rotwein ist sehr gut.

◆ Er ist wirklich vollmundig.

● Hat Ihnen der Schweinebraten geschmeckt?

◆ Er hat mir sehr gut geschmeckt – perfekt zubereitet!

● Hast du die Champignoncremesuppe probiert?

◆ Sie ist mir ein bisschen zu salzig.

● Zu salzig – absolut nicht! Die Suppe schmeckt fantastisch!

● Was hältst du von dem Apfelstrudel?

◆ Perfekt ... ich glaube, er enthält Rum, oder?

a 4; b 5; c 1; d 3; e 2

3 ● Was hältst du von dem Apfelstrudel?

◆ Perfekt! Nicht zu süß. Ich glaube, er enthält Rum, oder? Er erinnert mich an den Strudel meiner Tante. Früher hat sie ihn zum Geburtstag meines Onkels gebacken. Jedes Jahr. Wir haben früher den Strudel mit Vanillesoße gegessen und dazu Sekt getrunken.

Wer? Julia's aunt used to make it. Wann? Every year for her uncle's birthday.

Page 99

2 ● Also, Kompliment an den Chefkoch und an die Klasse von 2012. Es war ein fantastisches Essen. Fantastisch. Es ist ausgezeichnet gelaufen. Die Vorspeise war perfekt – ein Meisterwerk.

◆ Einen Toast auf den Chefkoch und die Köche!

● Auf die Köche!

◆ Und jetzt bereitet es mir große Freude, Claudia einen herzlichen Glückwunsch zum Geburtstag zu wünschen. Claudia – wir gratulieren! Herzlichen Glückwunsch!

a fantastisch (splendid); b first course (Champignoncremesuppe); c the head chef and the cooks; d Claudia

3 Cooking a German meal; matching food and wine; learning a lot of German

Page 100 Put it all together

1 *a 4; b 5; c 8; d 6; e 1; f 7; g 2; h 3*

2 *c, b, a, f, e, d*

3 werde kochen – future; habe geschlafen – perfect; hatte – imperfect; rufe ... an – present; bin gegangen – perfect; wohne – present; werde arbeiten – future; habe gegessen – perfect; werde beenden – future; war – imperfect; habe geglaubt – perfect

Page 101 Now you're talking!

1 ● Schmeckt dir die Erbsensuppe?
  ◆ **Sie ist fantastisch, perfekt zubereitet.**
  ● Du musst diese Mohnbrötchen probieren. Sie schmecken so gut.
  ◆ **Ja, sie sind sehr gut. Hast du die Sesambrötchen probiert?**
  ● Die Sesambrötchen schmecken mir am besten. Aber dieses Brot hier ist auch gut ... Und was hältst du von dem Wein?
  ◆ **Er ist fantastisch, so leicht und fruchtig. Er schmeckt mir.**
  ● Die deutschen Weine sind gut, nicht wahr?
  ◆ **Mir hat der Aperitif, der Sekt, sehr gut geschmeckt.**

2 ● **Was für ein schöner Kuchen!**
  ◆ Ich habe ihn nach einem Rezept meiner Großmutter gebacken. Er enthält Mandeln. Sind Sie allergisch gegen Nüsse?
  ● **Nein, ich bin nicht allergisch gegen Nüsse.**
  ◆ Was halten Sie von dem Kuchen?
  ● **Er schmeckt mir sehr gut; er erinnert mich an ein englisches Rezept. Kompliment an den Chefkoch!**

  ◆ Morgen gebe ich Ihnen das Rezept.
  ● **Herzlichen Dank, Fabian. Ich hatte so viel Spaß. Auf Wiedersehen.**
  ◆ Auf Wiedersehen.

Page 102 Quiz

*1 Wasser; 2 schmecken; 3 geröstet (roast); 4 Der Wein ist nicht nur leicht, sondern auch fruchtig; 5 **Früher** habe ich viel gekocht; 6 red wine; 7 die Suppe wird gekocht; 8 Kompliment an den Chefkoch!*

braten – in einer Pfanne kochen; Karfoffelknödel – eine Sorte von Knödel, die Kartoffeln enthält; Dornfelder– ein Rotwein; lieblich – ziemlich süß; ausgezeichnet – fantastisch/wunderbar

Noch mehr! 5

Pages 103-106

1 *a richtig; b falsch; c richtig; d falsch; e falsch; f richtig; g richtig; h richtig.*

2 **Land, in dem sich das Haus befindet:** England
  Immobilientyp: neues Einfamilienhaus
  Anzahl der Schlafzimmer: 4
  Anzahl der Badezimmer: 3
  Merkmale der Immobilie: Garten ✓; Terrasse ✓; Balkon ✗; Klimaanlage ?; Garage/Stellplatz ✓; Panoramablick ✓; Privatpool ✗; Zentralheizung ✓
  Ausstattung: moderne Küche ✓; Fernseher ?; Aufzug ✗; Spülmaschine ?; Internetanschluss ?; Kamin ✓
  In der Nähe: Geschäfte ✓; Strand ?; öffentliches Schwimmbad ✓; Sportzentrum ?; Restaurants ✓; Spielplatz ✓; öffentliche Transportmittel ✓; Golfplatz ✓

3 *a*
  ● Willkommen in Deutschland. Ich heiße Elke.
  ◆ **Freut mich. Ich heiße Rob. Meine Frau ist nicht hier. Sie ist in die Stadt gegangen.**
  ● Wie heißt Ihre Frau?
  ◆ **Sie heißt Samira.**
  ● Gefällt Ihnen Schleswig-Holstein?

◆ **Es gefällt mir sehr – es ist so schön und interessant.**
● Sind Sie zum ersten Mal in Deutschland?
◆ **Vor zwei Jahren waren wir in Berlin. Letztes Jahr sind wir nach Frankreich gefahren – aber ich mag Deutschland lieber. Ich liebe Deutschland; seit zwei Jahren lerne ich Deutsch.**

b
● Also, was haben Sie bis jetzt in Schleswig-Holstein gesehen?
◆ **Am Montag bin ich alleine nach Lübeck gefahren, wo ich das Holstentor besucht habe. Es hat mir sehr gut gefallen.**
● Wie war das Wetter?
◆ **Es war heiß.**
● Wann sind Sie abgefahren?
◆ **Ich bin um acht Uhr morgens abgefahren.**
● Und was haben Sie am Dienstag gemacht?
◆ **Wir sind nach Travemünde gefahren, wo wir das Seebadmuseum besucht haben.**
● Haben Sie das Maritim Hochhaus gesehen?
◆ **Ja, wir haben es gesehen, aber wir haben es leider nicht fotografiert, weil wir unsere Kamera verloren haben.**

● Wie schade! Haben Sie eine Anzeige gemacht?
◆ **Ja, wir sind zum Polizeirevier in Lübeck gegangen.**
● Noch ein Glas Wein, Rob?
◆ **Nein, danke. Wir hatten viel Spaß, aber wir müssen jetzt gehen. Herzlichen Dank!**
● Bitte – keine Ursache! Bis nächstes Jahr!

4 Liebe Maria,
Wir sind am Samstag in Deutschland angekommen. Wir wohnen in einem großen Einfamilienhaus in Lübeck. Es gibt einen Supermarkt in der Nähe, und wir haben eine kleine Kneipe gefunden. Am Sonntag war es sehr warm. Wir stehen jeden Morgen früh auf.
Wir sind am Montag nach Lübeck gefahren. Rob hat das Holstentor besucht, und ich habe eine Menge eingekauft!
Wir haben hier eine tolle Aussicht. Aber wir haben keine Fotos, weil Rob am Dienstag die Kamera verloren hat. Wir haben im Polizeirevier eine Verlustanzeige gemacht. Dann haben wir die falsche Straße genommen und sind erst nach Mitternacht zurückgekehrt!
Es war wunderbar … und nächstes Jahr kommen wir wieder nach Deutschland.
Liebe Grüße
Samira

pronunciation and spelling

1 German vowels and vowels with umlauts are either long or short:

	a	ä	e	i	o	ö	u	ü
long	Banane	fährt	den	mir	rot	schön	gut	über
short	Hand	hätte	elf	ist	Osten	möchte	Mund	nützlich

h after a vowel lengthens the sound: z**eh**n; a double vowel is also a long sound: **Staat** *state*. Double or multiple consonants after a vowel shorten the sound: **Zimmer, füllen, Hand, Rest**.

2 Diphthongs

	English sound	Examples
au	*ow* in *how*	Haus
äu/ eu	*oi* in *oil*	Häuser, Europa
ei	*i* in *fine*	Wein
ie	*ee* in *bee*	Bier

3 **Consonants** other than these sound very similar in German and English:

	English sound	Examples
c	*k* before **a, o, u**; *ts* before **e, i**	Camping, Celsius
ch	Scottish *ch* after **a, o, u, au**	acht, Buch
	h in *huge* after **e, i, ä, ö, ü** and consonants	ich, München
g	hard *g* in *good*	Geld, Magen *stomach*
j	*y* in *year*	Jahr, jeder
qu	*kv*	Qualität, Quiz
r	*r* but hard and guttural	Regen, Bremen
s	*z*	sechs, sieben
sch	*sh*	schön, vermischen *to mix*
sp	*shp* at the beginning of words (otherwise as English)	Sport, spielen
st	*sht* at the begining of words (otherwise as English)	Straße, Stunde
v	*f*	vier, von
w	*v*	Wein, wohnen
x	*ks*	Mixer, Axt *axe*
z	*ts*	zehn, Zoo

4 **ß**, the equivalent of **ss**, comes after long vowels and diphthongs.

5 **h** is pronounced at the beginning of a word, but is not pronounced when used to lengthen a vowel, as in 1, or at the end of a word.

6 **e** at the end of a word is never silent and sounds like the final *er* of *better*.

numbers and dates

0 null	15 fünfzehn	30 dreißig*
1 eins	16 sechzehn	40 vierzig
2 zwei	17 siebzehn	50 fünfzig
3 drei	18 achtzehn	60 sechzig
4 vier	19 neunzehn	70 siebzig
5 fünf	20 zwanzig	80 achtzig
6 sechs	21 einundzwanzig	90 neunzig
7 sieben	22 zweiundzwanzig	100 hundert
8 acht	23 dreiundzwanzig	200 zweihundert
9 neun	24 vierundzwanzig	1.000 tausend
10 zehn	25 fünfundzwanzig	2.000 zweitausend
11 elf	26 sechsundzwanzig	1.000.000 eine Million
12 zwölf	27 siebenundzwanzig	2.000.000 zwei Millionen
13 dreizehn	28 achtundzwanzig	
14 vierzehn	29 neunundzwanzig	

* 31 to 99 follow the same pattern as 21 to 29: **einunddreißig, zweiunddreißig, dreiunddreißig**, etc.

1st erste**	6th sechste
2nd zweite	7th siebte
3rd dritte	8th achte
4th vierte	9th neunte
5th fünfte	10th zehnte

** For ordinal numbers after 10th, **-te** is added to the number; for numbers after 19th, **-ste** is added: 20th **zwanzigste**, 31st **einunddreißigste**. Ordinal number have adjectival endings: **der zehnte**, **am vierten**.

Montag *Monday*	**Freitag** *Friday*
Dienstag *Tuesday*	**Samstag,**
Mittwoch *Wednesday*	**Sonnabend** *Saturday*
Donnerstag *Thursday*	**Sonntag** *Sunday*

Januar *January*	**Juli** *July*
Februar *February*	**August** *August*
März *March*	**September** *September*
April *April*	**Oktober** *October*
Mai *May*	**November** *November*
Juni *June*	**Dezember** *December*

Days and months are all masculine. Dates are written **3. August** and said **Dritter August.**

grammar

This section uses the key grammatical terms defined on page 6.

G1 **Nouns** are written with a capital letter in German: **Er trinkt ein Glas Wein und isst einen grünen Salat**.

G2 **Gender:** Nouns are all either masculine (m), feminine (f) or neuter (n). It's a good strategy to learn the gender of every noun you come across because it usually isn't obvious. However, the gender of some can be deduced from their meaning or ending:

masculine: ending in **-ant**, **-ig**, **-ich**, **-ling**, **-or**, **-ast**, **-ismus**, **-us**; seasons and months; days of the week; male people and animals; points of the compass; weather words; rocks and precious stones; alcoholic drinks (except **das Bier**); makes of car; rivers outside Germany;

feminine: ending in **-a**, **-age**, **anz**, **-e**, **-ei**, **-enz**, **-heit**, **-keit**, **-schaft**, **-ie**, **-ik**, **-in**, **-sis**, **-sion**, **-tion**, **-tät**, **-ung**, **-ur**; female people; rivers in Germany (except **der Rhein**); most trees, fruits, and flowers;

neuter: ending in **-chen**, **-it**, **-il**, **-lein**, **-icht**, **ma**, **tel**, **-tum**, **-ment**, **-ium**, **-um**; metals and chemical elements; letters of the alphabet; verbs used as nouns; towns, provinces and most countries.

Compound nouns take the gender of the last noun: e.g. **der Bahnhof** (**die Bahn**, <u>der</u> **Hof**).

G3 **Plurals:** There are a few rules in forming the plural of nouns, but also many exceptions, so it's also best to learn a new noun with its plural form.

In general, many masculine nouns form their plural by adding **-e**, while neuter nouns form theirs by adding **-er**. In both instances, an umlaut is added to the vowels **a**, **o** or **u**. Feminine nouns form their plural with **-(e)n**.

G4 The four **cases** relate to the different roles that a noun or pronoun plays in a sentence.

Nominative: subject of the sentence, carrying out the verb;

Accusative: direct object of the verb, directly affected by it. Also used after certain prepositions.

Dative: indirect object of the verb, affected by it but indirectly. The English translation often includes *to*. Also used after certain prepositions and verbs such as **geben**, **helfen** and **folgen**.

Genitive: relating to possession. It is also used after a few prepositions: **das Alter des Mädchens** *the girl's age*; **wegen des Regens** *because of the rain*; **während des Filmes** *during the film*.

Case affects the ending of any words used with a noun, such as articles and adjectives. And in the dative plural, as well as the genitive singular of masculine and neuter nouns, the noun itself adds an ending: **Er spielt mit den Kindern**; **Sie gibt den Hunden Wasser**.

G5 **Articles:** In English, the only definite article is *the*, and the indefinite article is *a/an*. In German, both definite (**der**, **die**, **das**) and indefinite (**ein**, **eine**) articles have different forms according to the gender and case of the noun they're with. *The* also has forms for use with plural nouns.

	masculine	feminine	neuter	plural
nominative	**der** **ein**	**die** **eine**	**das** **ein**	**die**
accusative	**den** **einen**	**die** **eine**	**das** **ein**	**die**
dative	**dem** **einem**	**der** **einer**	**dem** **einem**	**den -n**[1]
genitive	**des -(e)s**[2] **eines -(e)s**	**der** **einer**	**des-(e)s** **eines -(e)s**	**der**

[1] **-n** is added to the plural noun form, e.g. **Kinder** (pl) – **Kindern** (dative, pl)

[2] **-s** is added to the singular form of nouns of more than one syllable: **Zimmer** – **Zimmers** *of the room*; short nouns of only one syllable need an **-es** ending: **Mann** – **Mannes** *of the man*

G6 **Adjectives** An adjective after a noun is always in the dictionary form. But an adjective *before* a noun adds an ending, so that it agrees in gender, number (singular or plural) and case with that noun. The endings are slightly different after the definite and indefinite articles.

1 Adjective endings after the definite article:

	masculine	feminine	neuter	plural
nominative	**der große Mann**	**die große Frau**	**das große Kind**	**die großen Männer**
accusative	**den großen Mann**	**die große Frau**	**das große Kind**	**die großen Männer**
dative	**dem großen Mann**	**der großen Frau**	**dem großen Kind**	**den großen Männern**
genitive	**des großen Mannes**	**der großen Frau**	**des großen Kindes**	**der großen Männer**

2 Adjective endings after the indefinite article:

	masculine	feminine	neuter	plural
nominative	ein großer Mann	eine große Frau	ein großes Kind	keine* großen Männer
accusative	einen großen Mann	eine große Frau	ein großes Kind	keine großen Männer
dative	einem großen Mann	einer großen Frau	einem großen Kind	keinen großen Männern
genitive	eines großen Mannes	einer großen Frau	eines großen Kindes	keiner großen Männer

* As there is no plural of **ein**, **kein** *no*, *none* is used to demonstrate the endings.

3 Adjective endings without an article:

	masculine	feminine	neuter	plural
nominative	deutscher Wein	deutsche Wurst	deutsches Bier	deutsche Filme
accusative	deutschen Wein	deutsche Wurst	deutsches Bier	deutsche Filme
dative	deutschem Wein	deutscher Wurst	deutschem Bier	deutschen Filmen
genitive	deutschen Weines	deutscher Wurst	deutschen Bieres	deutscher Filme

G7 **Adverbs:** In German, most adjectives can be used as adverbs, without the need for any changes: **Die Musik ist laut.** *The music is loud.* **Sie singt laut.** *She sings loudly.* Word order with adverbs is sometimes the same as it is in English: **Er fährt langsam durch den Schnee.** *He drives slowly through the snow.* However, in German an adverb cannot go between the subject and verb: **Er kennt sicher den Chefkoch.** *He surely knows the chef.* Normally the adverb follows the verb but sometimes it begins the sentence. The verb usually comes second: **Glücklicherweise ist es heute sonnig.** *Fortunately it is sunny today.*

G8 **Comparative and superlative:** When making comparisons, adjectives and adverbs add **-er**. Most adjectives and adverbs of one syllable and containing **a**, **o** or a **u** also add an umlaut. **Gesund** (adj and adv): **Orangen sind gesünder** (adj) **als Kuchen.** *Oranges are healthier than cake.* **Ich lebe jetzt gesünder** (adv). *I live more healthily now.*

Than is **als**, which is followed by the nominative: **Sie ist größer als der Mann.**

The German equivalent of the English -est ending (the superlative) on an adjective is -(e)ste plus the appropriate adjective ending.
Sie ist die älteste, aber die kleinste in der Klasse.
Ich möchte den größten Kuchen kaufen.

The superlative of an adverb starts with **am** and adds -(e)sten: **er singt am schönsten.**

G9 The possessive adjectives are **mein** *my*, **dein** *your* (**du**), **sein** *his/its*, **ihr** *her*, **unser** *our*, **euer** *your* (**ihr**), **Ihr** *your* (**Sie**)

They have to agree with the case of the following noun and take the same endings as **ein** *a/an*: **Er ruft seinen Bruder an; Meine Schwester besucht ihren Schwiegervater**. When **euer** takes an ending, its second **e** is dropped: **ich mag euren Hund.**

G10 Demonstrative adjectives and pronouns

When **dieser/diese/dieses** and all their related forms (they have the same endings as the definite article) are used before a noun, they can mean *this* or *that*, or *these* or *those* and are referred to as <u>demonstrative adjectives</u>: **Wir mögen diesen Film./Ich kaufe diese Karte.**

	masculine	feminine	neuter	plural
nominative	dieser Mann	diese Frau	dies(es) Kind	diese Leute
accusative	diesen Mann	diese Frau	dies(es) Kind	diese Leute
dative	diesem Mann	dieser Frau	diesem Kind	diesen Leuten
genitive	dieses Mannes	dieser Frau	dieses Kindes	dieser Leute

When these forms are used on their own, they can mean *this one*, *that one*, *these (ones)* or *those (ones)* and are referred to as <u>demonstrative pronouns</u>. When the meaning is *that one*, *those ones* etc, **da** *there* is often added for clarification: **Dieser da ist sehr schön.** The neuter form **dieses** is often abbreviated to **dies** in the nominative and accusative cases: **Dies(es) ist mein Lieblingsbuch** *favourite book*.

G11 Expressing *it* in German

As all nouns are masculine, feminine or neuter, the gender has to be expressed when using the pronouns *it* and *them* in German. There are four different forms (including the plural *them*) in three cases.

	nominative	accusative	dative
masculine	er	ihn	ihm
feminine	sie	sie	ihr
neuter	es	es	ihm
plural	sie	sie	ihnen

Personal pronouns

nominative (subject pronoun)	accusative (direct object pronoun)	dative (indirect object pronoun)
ich *I*	**mich** *me*	**mir** *(to) me*
du *you*	**dich** *you*	**dir** *(to) you*
er *he*	**ihn** *him*	**ihm** *(to) him*
sie *she*	**sie** *her*	**ihr** *(to) her*
es *it*	**es** *it*	**ihm** *(to) it*
wir *we*	**uns** *us*	**uns** *(to) us*
ihr *you*	**euch** *you*	**euch** *(to) you*
sie *they*	**sie** *them*	**ihnen** *(to) them*
Sie *you*	**Sie** *you*	**Ihnen** *(to) you*

G13 **Relative pronouns** are the words used to introduce another clause (a 'subordinate clause') which refers back to a particular concept (usually a noun) in the main clause. The relative pronoun must agree in number and gender with the person or thing it refers back to. In the following sentence, **Der Mann ist mein Vater** is the main clause and **den ich jeden Tag sehe** is the subordinate clause. The relative pronoun **den** is masculine because it refers back to **Der Mann**:
Der Mann, den ich jeden Tag sehe, ist mein Vater. *The man, who I see every day, is my father.*

The case the relative pronoun takes is dependent on the role it plays within the relative clause. In the example, **den** is in the accusative: it is the direct object of the clause.

	masculine	feminine	neuter	plural
nominative	**der**	**die**	**das**	**die**
accusative	**den**	**die**	**das**	**die**
dative	**dem**	**der**	**dem**	**denen**
genitive	**dessen**	**deren**	**dessen**	**deren**

G14 **Prepositions** are followed by the accusative, dative or genitive.

Prepositions followed by the accusative include **bis** *until*; **durch** *through*; **entlang** *along*; **für** *for*; **gegen** *against*; **ohne** *without*; **um** *around, at* (time).

Prepositions followed by the dative include **aus** *from, out of*; **bei** *at*; **gegenüber** *opposite*; **mit** *with*; **nach** *after, to*; **seit** *since*; **von** *from, of*; **zu** *to* (**zu** combines with **dem** and **der** to give **zum** and **zur**).

Prepositions followed by the accusative and dative:

The prepositions opposite are followed by the accusative when motion is involved, and by the dative when location is described.

an	*on, at* (merges with **dem** and **das** to give **am/ans**)
auf	*on, onto*
in	*in, into* (merges with **dem** and **das** to give **im/ins**)
hinter	*behind*
neben	*near, next to, beside*
über	*over, above, across*
unter	*under, among*
vor	*in front of, before*
zwischen	*between*

Ich lege das Buch auf den Tisch. *I place the book on the table.* (acc.)
Das Buch liegt auf dem Tisch. *The book is lying on the table.* (dat.)

Prepositions followed by the genitive: **(an)statt** *instead of*, **außerhalb** *outside*, **innerhalb** *inside*, **trotz** *in spite of*, **während** *during*, **wegen** *because of*

Verbs

G15 There are six **modal verbs** in German: **dürfen** (*may – to be allowed to*), **können** (*can – to be able to*), **mögen** (*to like*), **müssen** (*must – to have to*), **sollen** (*ought to*) and **wollen** (*to want to*). The verb that follows a modal must be in the infinitive and placed at the end of the sentence or clause:

Er muss sein Auto waschen. *He must wash his car.*

	dürfen	können	mögen	müssen	sollen	wollen
ich	darf	kann	mag	muss	soll	will
du	darfst	kannst	magst	musst	sollst	willst
er/sie/es	darf	kann	mag	muss	soll	will
wir	dürfen	können	mögen	müssen	sollen	wollen
ihr	dürft	könnt	mögt	müsst	sollt	wollt
sie/Sie	dürfen	können	mögen	müssen	sollen	wollen

G16 **Reflexive verbs** always include an accusative or dative reflexive pronoun, which is rarely translated into English but which equates to:

- *myself, yourself*, etc (acc.) **Er rasiert sich**. *He shaves (himself).*

- *to myself, to yourself*, etc (dat.) **Ich überlege mir ein neues Spiel**. *I am thinking (to myself) about a new game.*

G17 **Reflexive pronouns** are the same as ordinary direct and indirect object pronouns (G12) apart from **sich** for all 3rd persons, singular and plural. Here are the patterns for **sich amüsieren** *to enjoy oneself* and **sich merken** *to memorise/remember* (lit. *to commit something <u>to</u> one's memory*):

ich amüsiere mich
du amüsierst dich
er/sie/es amüsiert sich
wir amüsieren uns
ihr amüsiert euch
sie/Sie amüsieren sich

ich merke mir
du merkst dir
er/sie/es merkt sich
wir merken uns
ihr merkt euch
sie/Sie merken sich

The majority of reflexive verbs need accusative reflexive pronouns; only a few need dative pronouns, of which the most common are:

sich vorstellen	*to imagine*
sich etwas einbilden	*to imagine wrongly*
sich weh tun	*to hurt oneself*
sich vorkommen	*to appear, to seem*

e.g. **Ich tue mir weh.**

Some others need a dative reflexive pronoun but also a direct object:

sich etwas anhören	*to listen to something*
sich etwas ansehen	*to look at/watch something*
sich etwas vorstellen	*to imagine something*
sich etwas ausleihen	*to borrow something*

e.g. **Siehst du dir den Film an?**

G18 **Verbs with separable prefixes**, e.g. **ankommen** *to arrive*, have their prefix attached in the infinitive but separate in the present and imperfect tense, when the prefix moves to the end of the clause/ sentence: **Ich komme am Montag an**. When the prefix is attached (e.g. in the past participle, see G20), the stress of the word is on the prefix. The prefixes are often words in their own right, e.g. **an**, **ab**, **vor**, **aus**. Separable verbs can be weak or strong (see G20).

G19 **Verbs with inseparable prefixes** always keep their prefix attached. Inseparable prefixes are **be-**, **emp-**, **ent-**, **er-**, **ge-**, **miss-**, **ver-**, **zer**, which are not words in their own right. These prefixes are not stressed. Inseparable verbs can be weak or strong (see G20).

G20 **Tenses**

The **present tense** is the equivalent of do, *am/is/are doing*. With **seit**, it means *have been doing*: **Ich arbeite seit sechs Monaten in Berlin.**

Weak verbs (also known as **regular verbs**) follow the pattern shown below:

If the stem of the verb, i.e. the main part of the verb without the -**(e)n** infinitive ending, ends in -**t** or -**d**, an **e** is added between the stem and the ending in the 2nd and 3rd person singular and 2nd person plural.

If the stem of the verb ends in -s, -z, -ß or -x, the ending in the 2nd person singular loses its s: **du reist** (**reisen** *to travel*).

	machen	arbeiten	reisen
ich	mache	arbeite	reise
du	machst	arbeitest	reist
er/sie/es	macht	arbeitet	reist
wir	machen	arbeiten	reisen
ihr	macht	arbeitet	reist
sie/Sie	machen	arbeiten	reisen

Strong verbs have exactly the same endings in the present tense but many of them undergo a stem change in the **du** and **er/sie/es** forms. The following verbs are common strong verbs:

	essen	fahren	geben	helfen	lesen	nehmen	sehen	sprechen
ich	esse	fahre	gebe	helfe	lese	nehme	sehe	spreche
du	isst	fährst	gibst	hilfst	liest	nimmst	siehst	sprichst
er/sie/es	isst	fährt	gibt	hilft	liest	nimmt	sieht	spricht
wir	essen	fahren	geben	helfen	lesen	nehmen	sehen	sprechen
ihr	esst	fahrt	gebt	helft	lest	nehmt	seht	sprecht
sie/Sie	essen	fahren	geben	helfen	lesen	nehmen	sehen	sprechen

Some strong verbs, e.g. **schreiben**, are regular in the present tense; the changes in stem appear in other tenses.

A few verbs (**irregular verbs**) are completely unpredictable: **haben**, **sein**, **wissen**, **werden** and the modal verbs (e.g. **dürfen**).

	haben	sein	wissen	werden	dürfen
ich	habe	bin	weiß	werde	darf
du	hast	bist	weißt	wirst	darfst
er/sie/es	hat	ist	weiß	wird	darf
wir	haben	sind	wissen	werden	dürfen
ihr	habt	seid	wisst	werdet	dürft
sie/Sie	haben	sind	wissen	werden	dürfen

The **imperative** forms of a verb are used to express commands, orders and requests. There are different imperative forms for **du**, **ihr** and **Sie**.

Besuche mich! (du) *Visit me!* (The **-e** ending is often omitted: **Besuch mich!**)
Besucht mich! (ihr) *Visit me!*
Besuchen Sie mich! (*you*, formal, sing and pl) *Visit me!*
In the **du** and **ihr** forms, the personal pronouns are omitted.

The **perfect tense** is the equivalent of *did* and *have done*. Most verbs form the perfect tense with the present tense of **haben** + the past participle of the main verb. A few verbs use the present tense of **sein** instead of **haben**. The majority of these are those that indicate motion towards a place, e.g. **fahren**, **kommen**, **gehen**; in addition there are those verbs that indicate a change of state, e.g. **sterben – gestorben**, and the verb **werden – geworden**.

The **past participle** can be formed in various ways, depending on the type of verb.

Weak/regular verbs: the past participle is formed by taking the infinitive, replacing the -**en** ending with -**t** and adding the prefix **ge-** to the beginning, e.g. **machen – gemacht**.

Verbs ending in -ieren in the infinitive: the infinitive ending is replaced with -**t**, but no prefix is necessary, e.g. **telefonieren – telefoniert**.

Strong verbs: the past participle ends in -**(e)n**. Many strong verbs undergo a stem change in the past participle, e.g. **gehen – gegangen**.

Irregular verbs: the past participles of irregular verbs usually end in -**en** but must be learned, as they don't follow a particular pattern: **wissen – gewusst**.

Separable verbs: the -**ge**- of the past participle goes between the separable prefix at the beginning and the main verb at the end, e.g: **ausfüllen – ausgefüllt; ankommen – angekommen**.

Inseparable verbs: the past participles of inseparable verbs never have an added **ge-** prefix: **bekommen – bekommen; verlieren – verloren; gehören – gehört**.

Imperfect tense forms are usually only used for more formal, mainly written, language. However, while the perfect tense is used in everyday language to refer to the past, it is more common to use **haben**, **sein**, **werden** and all modal verbs in the imperfect: **Gestern war** (imperfect) **ich in Berlin und habe dort ein neues Buch gekauft** (perfect).

G21 Word order

In a main clause, the verb must be the second idea. In a compound tense, such as the perfect tense, or if a modal verb is used, the two verb parts are separated, so that the first verb forms the second idea and the second verb goes to the end.

Der Kellner bringt eine Tasse Kaffee. (first idea: the waiter; second idea: the verb **bringt**)

Sie hat ein Geschenk *present* **gekauft.** (first idea: she; second idea: the verb **hat**; in final position: past participle **gekauft**)

Die junge Frau kann Deutsch sprechen. (first idea: the young woman; second idea: the modal verb **kann**; in final position: infinitive form **sprechen**)

Sometimes, a sentence starts with information other than the subject – usually information about time or place. The verb must always be the second idea, so the subject and verb swap places. This is called inversion.

Ich fahre nach Berlin.
Am Montag fahre ich nach Berlin.

Position of adverbs: when the sentence contains a lot of additional information in the form of adverbs, the order of the adverbs is time – manner – place. If any element is missing, the order remains the same:

Wir fahren morgen (time) **mit dem Zug** (manner) **nach Mannheim** (place).
Ich möchte nächstes Jahr (time) **nach Amerika** (place) **fliegen**.

Coordinating conjunctions are those joining words that link main clauses together but do not change the word order. These are: **aber**, **denn**, **oder**, **und**, **sondern**.

Er fährt in die Schweiz, und er besucht auch Italien.
Sie steht spät auf, aber sie geht immer früh ins Bett.

Subordinate clauses: subordinating conjunctions join sentences but change the word order. The main verb of the subordinate clause goes to the end of the clause and the rest of the clause remains the same.

Ich muss etwas essen. Ich habe Hunger.
Ich muss etwas essen, weil ich Hunger habe.

If there are two verbs in the subordinate clause, it is the first verb that goes in final position.

Ich bin krank. Ich habe zu viel gegessen.
Ich bin krank, weil ich zu viel gegessen <u>habe</u>.

Other common subordinating conjunctions are: **als** *when* (when used in connection with a past tense); **bis** *until*; **dass** *that*; **ob** *whether, if*; **obwohl** *although*; **während** *while*; **wenn** *when, if*

The same rules apply to relative clauses:
Er spricht mit der Frau, die er jeden Tag <u>sieht</u>.

German–English glossary

This glossary contains the words found in this book, with their meanings in the contexts used here. Most verbs are given only in the infinitive, but parts of some irregular German verbs are also included. (Pl) next to a noun means that the word occurs mostly or always in the plural. Abbreviations: (m) masculine, (f) feminine, (n) neuter, (sing) singular, (pl) plural, (pp) past participle, (adj) adjective, (nom.) nominative, (acc.) accusative, (dat.) dative, (gen.) genitive.

A

Abend (m) evening
Abendessen (n) supper
abends in the evening
aber but
abgelegen isolated, remote
abnehmen to lose weight
absolut absolute(ly)
Abstellraum (m) box room, utility room
Akkupunktur (f) acupuncture
aktiv active
Aktivurlaub (m) activity holiday
Alkohol (m) alcohol
alle all, every
Allee (f) avenue
alleine alone, on one's own
allergisch gegen allergic to
alles all, everything
Alpen (pl) Alps
als as, than, when
also well (then)
alt old
Altbau (m) old building
altmodisch old-fashioned
Altstadt (f) old town
am = an dem on (the) (day)
am besten best (of all)
am liebsten best of all, like … best
Amerika (n) America
Amerikaner(in) (m/f) American national
Ampel (f) traffic lights
sich amüsieren to enjoy oneself
an (acc./dat.) on/at
Anbaugebiet (n) growing area
andere(r) (f/m) other
Anfrage (f) request, enquiry
Angebot (n) offer

Angelegenheit (f) matter, concern
angeln to fish, to angle
angespannt tense
Angst haben to be scared
anprobieren to try on
Anrufbeantworter (m) answer machine
anrufen to call (on the telephone)
Antwort (f) reply, answer
antworten to answer
Anzahl (f) number
Anzeige (f) report
sich anziehen to get dressed
Apfel (m) apple
Apfelstrudel (m) apple strudel
Apfelwein (m) cider
Apotheke (f) chemist's
Apotheker(in) (m/f) chemist (person)
Appetit (m) appetite
   Guten Appetit! Enjoy your meal!
Arbeit (f) work
arbeiten to work
Architektur (f) architecture
Arm (m) arm
arm poor
Arme(r) (f/m): du Arme(r) you (informal) poor thing
Ärmel (m) sleeve
Art (f) kind, type
Artikel (m) article
Arzt/Ärztin (m/f) doctor
Astrologie (f) astrology
atemberaubend breathtaking(ly)
attraktiv attractive
auch also, too
auf (acc./dat.) on (top of), onto; in

Aufenthalt (m) stay
   Guten Aufenthalt! Enjoy your stay!
aufstehen to get up
aufwachen to wake up
Aufzug (m) lift
Auge (n) eye
Augenblick (m) moment
Augentropfen (m pl) eye drops
aus (dat.) from, out of, (made) from
auseinanderfallen to fall apart
Ausflug (m) excursion, trip
ausfüllen to fill in
Ausgangspunkt (m) starting point
ausgehen to go out
ausgereift aged
ausgestattet equipped, fitted
ausgewogen balanced
ausgezeichnet superb(ly)
aussehen to look (like)
Außengelände (n) external area
Aussicht (f) view
Ausstattung (f) equipment, furnishings
aussteigen to get off (bus etc.)
Australien (n) Australia
Ausweis (m) identity card
Ausweispapiere (n pl) identity papers
Auto (n): **mit dem Auto** by car
Axt (f) axe

B

backen to bake
Bäckerei (f) bakery
Bad (n) bath

Badezimmer (n) bathroom
Bahn (f) rail, train
Bahnhof (m) station
bald soon
Banane (f) banana
Bankier(in) (m/f) banker
bauen to build
Bauernhof (m) farm
Bauernküche (f) farm kitchen
Baum (m) tree
Baumeister(in) (m/f) builder
Baumwolle (f) cotton
beabsichtigen ... zu to intend to
Bedarf (m): **nach Bedarf** as needed
beenden to finish, to end
Beere (f) berry
sich befinden to be situated
beginnen to begin
behandeln to treat
Behandlung (f) treatment
beherbergen to accommodate
bei (dat.) at, by
Bein (n) leg
bekannt für known for
bekommen to get, receive
beliebt popular
bequem comfortable
Beratung (f) consultation
Berg (m) mountain
Bergdorf (n) mountain village
Berghütte (f) mountain chalet/hut
Bergsee (m) mountain lake
Beruf (m): **von Beruf** by profession
beschreiben to describe
besichtigen to visit
Besitzer(in) (m/f) owner
besonders particularly
besser better
bestätigen to confirm
bestimmt particular, certain
besuchen to visit
Besucher(in) (m/f) visitor
Betreff (m) reference
Bett (n) bed
bewölkt cloudy

bewundern to admire
bezahlen to pay, to pay for something
Bier (n) beer
billig cheap
bin (from **sein**) (I) am
bis (acc.) until, as far as
  bis jetzt until now
  bis später until later
  bis zu up to
bisschen: ein bisschen a bit/little
bist (from **sein**) (you, informal, sing) are
bitte (schön) please; there you are; don't mention it
bitten um to ask for
blass pale
blau blue
bleiben to stay
Blick (m) view
blond blonde
Blume (f) flower
Boden (m) floor
Brasilien (n) Brazil
braten to fry
brauchen to need
braun brown
Brief (m) letter
Briefmarke (f) stamp
Brieftasche (f) wallet
Brille (f) glasses
bringen to bring
Broschüre (f) brochure
Brot (n) bread
Brötchen (n) bread roll
Bruder (m) brother
Buch (n) book
buchen to book, reserve
Buchhalter(in) (m/f) accountant
Bundesland (n) federal state
bunt bright
Bus (m) bus
Bushaltestelle (f) bus stop
Butter (f) butter

C

Campingplatz (m) campsite
Champignoncremesuppe (f) cream of mushroom soup
Chefkoch (m) head chef

Chirurg(in) (m/f) surgeon
Christus Christ
Cousin (m) male cousin
Cousine (f) female cousin

D

da sein to be there
Dänemark (n) Denmark
danke thank you
danken to thank
dann then
darf (from **dürfen**) (I, he/she/it) may
dass that
Daten (pl) data
Datum (n) date
dauern to last
dazu with it
defekt broken
dein, deine your, informal, sing
Delegierte(r) (f/m) delegate
delikat delicate
denn for, because
Design (n) design
deutsch German
Deutsch (n) German (language)
Deutsche(r) (f/m) German national
Deutschland (n) Germany
Diät (f) diet
Diätprogramm (n) diet programme
dich you (informal, sing, acc.)
dick fat
Diele (f) hall(way)
diese(r/s) (f/m/n) this, these, that, those
dir to you (informal, sing, dat.)
Disko (f) disco
diskutieren to discuss
doch: ja doch but yes, all right
Doktor(in) (m/f) doctor
Dokument (n) document
Dom (m) cathedral
Doppelschlafcouch (f) double sofa bed
Dorf (n) village
dort there
dorthin (lit. to) there
Dosis (f) dose

draußen outside
dreimal three times
du you (sing, informal)
dünn thin
dunkel dark
dunkelblau dark blue, navy
dunkelhaarig dark-haired
durch (acc.) through
Durchschnitt (m) average
dürfen to be allowed
to, may
Dusche (f) shower
sich duschen to have
a shower
sich duzen to say **du** to
each other

E
Ecke (f) corner
Ei (n) egg
Einbauschrank (m) built-in
wardrobe
Einfamilienhaus (n) one-
family house
Eingangshalle (f) entrance
hall
Eingangstür (f) entrance
door
einige some, a few
einkaufen gehen to go
shopping
Einkaufszentrum (n)
shopping centre
einladen to invite
Einladung (f) invitation
einmal once
einmalig unique
einnehmen to take
(medication)
Einwohner(in) (m/f)
inhabitant
Einzelbett (n) single bed
Eis (n) ice cream
Eltern (pl) parents
Elternschlafzimmer (n)
master bedroom
E-Mail (f) e-mail
emotional emotional(ly)
empfehlen to recommend
Emulsion (f) mix, emulsion
Ende (n) end
  am Ende at the end
Engländer(in) (m/f) English
national
englisch English

Englisch (n) English
(language)
Enkel (m) grandson
entdecken to discover
entfernt away
enthält (from **enthalten**)
(he/she/it) contains
enthalten to contain
entlang (acc.) along
sich entscheiden to decide
sich entschuldigen to
excuse oneself
  entschuldigen Sie (mich)
excuse me
sich entspannen to relax
enttäuscht disappointed
er he, it
Erbsensuppe (f) pea soup
Erdgeschoss (n) ground
floor
Ereignis (n) incident, event
erfahren to find out
erhalten to receive
erinnern an to remind
Erkältungssirup (m)
cold syrup
erklären to declare, explain
Erlebnis (n) adventure,
experience
erlernen to learn, to
acquire
Ermäßigung (f) discount
Ernährungsproblem (n)
nutritional problem
ernst serious
erreichen to reach
erst not until
Erwachsene(r) (f/m) adult
erwärmen to heat
es it
es gab there was/were
sich es gemütlich
machen to make oneself
comfortable
Essen (n) meal, dish, food
essen to eat
Etage (f) floor, storey
Etagenbett (n) bunk bed
etwa approximately
etwas a little, some,
something
euch you (informal, pl,
acc.), to you (informal, pl,
dat.)
euer, eure your (informal, pl)

europäisch European
existieren to exist
Ex-Mann (m) ex-husband
Extremsport (m) extreme
sports

F
fabelhaft fantastic(ally)
Fach (n) compartment
Fähre (f) ferry
fahren to travel, to go
Fahrrad (n): **mit dem**
Fahrrad by bike
Fahrradschloss (n) bike lock
Fahrradtour (f) bicycle tour
Fahrradverleih (m) bike
rental outlet
fährst (from **fahren**) (you,
informal, sing) travel, go
fährt (from **fahren**) (he/
she/it) travels, goes
fallen to fall
falsch false, wrong
Familie (f) family
fantastisch fantastic
Farbe (f) colour
Federball (m) badminton
Feier (f) party, celebration
Feinschmecker(in) (m/f)
gourmet
Ferienhaus (n) holiday
home
Ferienimmobilie (f)
holiday property
Ferienwohnung (f) holiday
flat
Fernglas (n) binoculars
fernsehen to watch TV
Fernseher (m) TV set
fertig ready
Fest (n) celebration, festival
fest sturdy
Fieber (n) fever
finden to find
Firma (f) company, firm
Fisch (m) fish
Fitnessstudio (n) gym
Fliege (f) fly, bow-tie
fliegen to fly
Flora und Fauna (f) wildlife
Flug (m) flight
Fluggesellschaft (f) airline
folgen to follow
folgende(r/s) (f/m/n)
following

formen to shape
Foto (n) photograph
Fotograf/in (m/f) photographer
Fotografie (f) photography
fotografieren to take photos
Frage (f) question
Frankreich (n) France
Frau (f) woman, Mrs
frei available, free
Freien: im Freien outdoors
Freizeit (f) spare time, leisure
Freizeitangebot (n) leisure activity
Fremdenverkehrsamt (n) tourist office
Freude (f): **Freude bereiten** to give joy, pleasure
Freund(in) (m/f) (boy)/(girl) friend
freundlich friendly, kind
freut mich pleased to meet you
Friseur(in) (m/f) hairdresser
froh happy
fröhlich cheerful
fruchtig fruity
früh early
früher earlier, used to
Frühkartoffeln (pl) new potatoes
Führerschein (m) driving licence
Führung (f) guided tour
füllen to fill
Fundbüro (n) lost property office
für (acc.) for
furchtbar dreadful
Fuß (m) foot
Fußball (m) football
Fußballspiel (n) football match

G

gab (from **geben**) (I, he/she/it) gave
Gang (m) course
gar nicht not at all
Garten (m) garden
Gästeschlafzimmer (n) guest room
Gastfamilie (f) host family

Gastronomie- und Weinführer (m) food and wine guide
Gaststätte (f) inn, restaurant
gebaut (from **bauen**) built
geben to give, to put
Gebiet (n) area, region
Gebirge (n) mountain range
geboren born
Gebrauch (m) use
gebrochen (from **brechen**) broken
Geburtsdatum (n) date of birth
Geburtsort (m) birthplace
Geburtstag (m) birthday
geehrte(r) (f/m) dear (formal) (lit. honoured)
gefallen: mir gefällt I like
Gefrierschrank (m) freezer
gegen (acc.) around (time), against
Gegend (f) surrounding area
gegenüber (dat.) opposite
gehackt chopped
gehen to go (on foot)
gehören to belong
gekauft bought (pp of **kaufen**)
gelb yellow
Geld (n) money, cash
  Geld abheben to withdraw money, cash
Geldautomat (m) cash machine
gelegen situated
Gelegenheit (f) opportunity
gemein mean
Gemüse (n) vegetables
gemütlich comfortable, cosy
genannt called
genau precise(ly), exact(ly)
  genauer gesagt more precisely (said)
genießen to enjoy
genug enough
geografisch geographical(ly)
geprellt bruised
geradeaus straight on
geräumig spacious

gern(e) like ... ing (lit. with pleasure)
geröstet roast, fried
Gesamtwert (m) total value
Geschäft (n) shop
Geschenk (n) present
Geschichte (f) history
geschieden divorced
Geschmack (m): **nach Geschmack** according to taste
gestern yesterday
gestresst stressed
gesund healthy/healthily
Gesundheitsgrund (m) health reason
Gesundheitswesen (n) National Health Service
Gewitter (n) thunderstorm
gibt (from **geben**): **es gibt** there is, there are
gießen to pour
Gipfel (m) peak, summit
Glas (n) glass
glatt straight
glauben to believe, to think
glücklich happy
  ihr Glücklichen! Lucky you!
glücklicherweise fortunately
Glückwunsch (m) congratulations
  Herzlichen Glückwunsch! Congratulations!
  Herzlichen Glückwunsch zum Geburtstag! Happy Birthday!
Grad (m) degree
Grafiker(in) (m/f) graphic designer
gratis free of charge
gratulieren to congratulate
grau grey
grenzen an to border on
Griechenland (n) Greece
Grillparty (f) barbecue party
Grippe (f) flu
groß big, large
Großbritannien (n) Great Britain
Größe (f) size
Großeltern (pl) grandparents

Großmutter (f) grandmother
Großstadt (f) city
Großvater (m) grandfather
grün green
gründen to found
Grüße (pl) greetings
  liebe Grüße love/kind regards (informal)
  mit freundlichen Grüßen best wishes
Grund (m): **aus diesem Grund** for this reason
Gruppe (f) group
gültig bis valid until
günstig good, favourable/ favourably
gut good
gutaussehend good-looking

H

haben to have
Hafen (m) harbour
Hafenstadt (f) harbour town
halb half
halbtrocken semi-dry
Halle (f) hall
Hals (m) throat
Halspastille (f) throat lozenge
Halsschmerzen (pl) sore throat
Haltestelle (f) (bus) stop
hältst ... von (from **halten von**) (you, informal, sing) think of
Hand (f) hand
  von Hand by hand
Handtuch (n) towel
Handy (n) mobile phone
Harmonie (f) harmony
hast (from **haben**) (you, informal, sing) have
hätte (from **haben**) I, he/she/it would have
hattest (from **haben**) (you, informal, sing) had
Hauptbahnhof (m) main train station
hauptsächlich mainly
Hauptspeise (f) main course
Haus (n) house
Hauterkrankung (f) skin disease

Heil- und Kurort (m) spa resort
Heilbad (n) health spa
Heilkräuter (pl) medicinal herbs
Heimat (f) home (town, land)
heiraten to marry, to get married
heiß hot
heißen to be called
helfen to help
hell light
hellblau light blue
hellbraun light brown
Helm (m) helmet
Hemd (n) shirt
Herbst (m) autumn
Herr (m) Mr
herrlich marvellous
herzlich cordial(ly), heartfelt
heute today, this (time of day)
hier here
hierher (lit. to) here
Hilfe (f) help
hinter (acc./dat.) behind
hinterlassen to leave (a message)
historisch historical(ly)
hoch high
Hochhaus (n) tower block
Hochzeitstag (m) wedding anniversary
Hof (m) yard
hoffen to hope
höflich polite
Höhe (f) height
holistisch holistic(ally)
Homöopathie (f) homeopathy
homöopathisch homeopathic
Hör mal! Listen!
hören to hear, to listen
Hose (f) trousers
Hotelführer (m) hotel guide
hügelig hilly
Hunger haben to be hungry
Husten (m) cough
Hustensaft (m) cough syrup
Hut (m) hat

Hydrotherapie (f) hydrotherapy

I

ich I
Idee (f) idea
idyllisch idyllic
ihm to him, to it
ihn him
ihnen to them
Ihnen to you (formal, sing and pl)
ihr to her; you (informal, pl)
ihr(e) her, their
Ihr(e) your (formal, sing and pl)
immer always
immer noch still
Immobilie (f) property
Immobilienmakler(in) (m/f) estate agent
Immobilientyp (m) type of property
in (acc./dat.) in
Informationsblatt (n) information leaflet
Inhalt (m) contents
inklusive inclusive
innere(r/s) inner
Insel (f) island
insgesamt altogether, in all
interessant interesting
sich interessieren für to be interested in
Internetanschluss (m) internet connection
Irak (m) Iraq
isst (from **essen**) (he/she/it/ you, informal) eat(s)
ist (from **sein**) is

J

ja yes
Jacke (f) jacket
Jahr (n) year
  bis nächstes Jahr until next year
  dieses Jahr this year
  in diesem Jahr this year
  jedes Jahr every year
  nächstes Jahr next year
Jahrhundert (n) century
japanisch Japanese
jede(r) (f/m) every
jemand someone

jetzt now
Journalist(in) (m/f) journalist
Jubiläum (n) anniversary
jung young

K

Kaffee (m) coffee
Kaffeepause (f) coffee break
Kalender (m) calendar
Kalorien (pl) calories
kalt cold
Kamera (f) camera
Kamin (m) fireplace
Kampfsport (m) martial arts
Kampfsportarten (pl) types of martial art
kanariengelb canary yellow
kann (from **können**) (I, he/she/it) can
　Kann ich mal sehen? Can I have a look?
Kapsel (f) capsule
Karibik (f) Caribbean
Karneval (m) Carnival
Karte (f) map
Kartoffel (f) potato
Kaschmir (m) cashmere
Kastanie (f) chestnut
Katastrophe (f) catastrophe
kaufen to buy
Kaution (f) deposit
Kegelbahn (f) bowling alley
kegeln to play ninepins/skittles
kein, keine no, none
Keller (m) basement, cellar
Kellner(in) waiter/waitress
kennen to know (people and places)
Kern (m) core, centre
Kilometer (m) kilometre
Kind (n) child
Kino (n) cinema
Klasse (f) class
Klassenkamerad (m) school friend
Kleid (n) dress
sich kleiden to dress (oneself)
klein small
Klempner(in) m/f plumber
Klimaanlage (f) air conditioning
Klimawandel (m) climate change (m)
Kloß (m) dumpling
Kneipe (f) pub
Knie (n) knee
Knöchel (m) ankle
Knödel (m) dumpling
Koch/Köchin (m/f) cook
kochen to cook, to boil
kochend boiling
Kochnische (f) kitchenette
komfortabel comfortable
kommen (he/she/it) to come
kommt ... an (from **ankommen**) (he, she, it) arrives
kompakt compact
komplett complete(ly), fully
Kompliment (n) compliments
Konferenz (f) conference
König (m) king
können to be able to, can
Kontakt (m) contact
Konversation (f) conversation
Konzert (n) concert
Kopf (m) head
Kopfschmerzen (pl) headache
Kopfschmerztabletten (pl) headache tablets
körperlich physical(ly)
kosten to cost
kostenlos free of charge
krank ill
Krankenhaus (n) hospital
Krawatte (f) tie
Kreditkarte (f) credit card
Küche (f) kitchen, cuisine
Kuchen (m) cake
Kühlschrank (m) refrigerator
Kultur (f) culture
Kunde (f) study of
Kung Fu machen to do kung fu
Kunst (f) art
Kurort (m) health resort
Kurs (m) course
Kurtourismus (m) spa tourism

kurz short
kurzum in short
Kurzurlaub (m) short break/vacation
Küste (f) coast

L

lächeln to smile
lächerlich ridiculous
Lage (f) location, situation
Land (n) country(side)
Landeshauptstadt (f) federal capital city
Landhaus (n) country house
lang long
langärmelig long-sleeved
langsam slow(ly)
lassen to leave (something behind), to lose, to let
laufen to go, to run, to walk
leben to live
Lebensmittelgeschäft (n) grocery store
Leder (n) leather
leicht light
leid: tut mir leid I am sorry
leiden an to suffer from
leider unfortunately
Leihgebühr (f) rental rate
Leinen (n) linen
lernen to learn
lesen to read
Libanon (m) Lebanon
lieb kind, sweet
liebe(r) dear
lieben to love
lieber rather, prefer (with verb)
lieblich sweet
Lieblings- favourite
liegen to lie, to be situated
links left
Liste (f) list
lockig curly
Löffel (m) spoon
lokal local
Lokalzeitung (f) local newspaper
los: Was ist los? What's the matter?
losfahren to set off
Lust haben auf to fancy
lustig funny, amusing
lutschen to suck

M

machen to make, do
mag (from **mögen**) (I/he/she/it) likes
Magen (m) stomach
Magenschmerzen (pl) stomach ache
Mahlzeit (f) meal
Mal (n): **zum ersten Mal** for the first time
mal sehen let's see
malen to paint
man one, you
manchmal sometimes
Mandel (f) almond
Mann (m) man, husband
Massagekunst (f) art of massage
Mauer (f) wall
Medikament (n) medication
Medizin (f) medicine
medizinisch medical(ly)
Meer (n) sea
mehr more, anymore
mein, meine my
mein Lieber/meine Liebe my dear (m/f)
meisten: die meisten the most
Meisterwerk (n) masterpiece
Menge: eine Menge a lot
Mensch (m) human being, person
Menstruationsprobleme (pl) menstruation problems
sich merken (dat.) to memorise, to remember
Merkmal (n) feature
Messe (f) trade show
Meter (m/n) metre
Metropole (f) metropolis
mich me
mieten to hire, rent
Mietshaus (n) block of flats
Milch (f) milk
Million (f) million
mindestens at least
Minister(in) (m/f) minister
mir to me
mit (dat.) with
 Mit (dem größten) Vergnügen (n) With (very great) pleasure

mitbringen to bring along
Mittagessen (n) lunch
mittags at lunchtime
mitteilen to tell, to inform
mittelalterlich medieval
Mitteleuropa (n) Central Europe
Mittelgebirge (n) Central German Uplands
mitten in the middle of
Mitternacht (f) midnight
möchte (from **mögen**) (I/he/she/it) would like
Mode (f) fashion
Modeindustrie (f) fashion industry
modisch fashionable
mögen to like
möglich possible
Mohnbrötchen (n) poppy seed roll
mollig chubby
Moment mal one moment
Monat (m) month
morgen tomorrow
morgens in the morning
müde tired
Mund (m) mouth
Musik (f) music
Musiker(in) (m/f) musician
muss (from **müssen**) (I, he/she/it) must
müssen to have to, must
Mutter (f) mother
Muttertag (m) Mother's Day

N

na ja well then
nach (dat.) to (town, country), past, after
 nach Hause home, to my/your etc. house
Nachbarhaus (n) house next door
Nachmittag (m) afternoon
nachmittags in the afternoon
Nachname (m) surname
Nachricht (f) message
Nachspeise (f) dessert
nächste(r) next
nachts at night
Nähe (f): **in der Nähe von** nearby

Nase (f) nose
Nasenloch (n) nostril
Nasenspray (m/n) nose spray
nass wet
Nationalität (f) nationality
natürlich of course, naturally
Natur (f) nature
Naturlehrwanderung (f) nature trail
Naturschutzgebiet (n) nature reserve
nebelig foggy
neben (acc./dat.) next to, beside, near
nehmen to take
nennen to call, to name
nett nice
neu new
Neubau (m) new-build
neugebaut newly built
Neugier (f): **aus Neugier** out of curiosity
nicht not
 nicht nur ... sondern auch not only ... but also
 nicht so ... not so ...
 nicht so (adj) **wie** not as (adj) as
 nicht wahr? isn't it, don't you, was it? etc.
nichts nothing
niemand no one
noch nicht not yet
noch nie never before
Norden (m) North
nördlich northerly
Nordsee (f) North Sea
normalerweise normally
Notarzt (m) emergency doctor
Notaufnahme (f) casualty department
nur only
Nuss (f) nut
Nüsse (pl) nuts
nützlich useful

O

ob if, whether
obwohl although
oder or
oder? doesn't it?, isn't it? etc.

Ofen (m) oven
öffentlich public
öffnen to open
Öffnungszeiten (pl) opening times
oft often
oh je oh dear
ohne (acc.) without
Ohr (n) ear
Ohrenschmerzen (pl) earache
Oma (f) grandma
Omelett (m) omelette
Onkel (m) uncle
Opernmusik (f) opera
Orange (f) orange
Ordnung (f): **in Ordnung** in order, okay
organisieren to organise
Ort (m) place, location
Osten (m) East
Österreich Austria
Ostsee (f) Baltic Sea

P

paar: ein paar a few, some
Panorama (n) panorama
Panoramablick (m) panoramic view
Paradies (n) paradise
Park (m) park
Partner(in) (m/f) partner
Pass (m) passport
passend matching
passieren to happen
Pause (f) break
pendeln to commute
perfekt perfect
persönlich personal(ly)
Petersilie (f) parsley
Pfanne (f) frying pan
Pfeffer (m) pepper
Pferd (m): **zu Pferd** on horseback
Planänderung (f) change of plan
planen to plan
Platz (m) square, place
Pole/Polin (m/f) Polish national
Polen (n) Poland
Polizei (f) police
Polizeirevier (n) police station
Polizist(in) (m/f) police officer

populär popular
Portemonnaie (n) purse
Portugiese/Portugiesin (m/f) Portuguese national
Portugiesisch Portuguese (language)
Postbote/Postbotin (m/f) postman/post woman
praktisch practical
Praxis (f) practice
Preis (m) price
Pressesprecher(in) (m/f) press officer
prima great
Privatpool (m) private pool
pro per
probieren to try, to taste
Problem (n) problem
Prosit! Cheers!
Prost! Cheers!
Prozent (n) per cent
Pullover (m) jumper
Pulver (n) powder
Punkt (m) point

Q

Qualität (f) quality
Qualitätswein (m) **mit Prädikat** (n) quality wine with distinction

R

Radweg (m) cycle path
sich rasieren to shave (oneself)
Rathaus (n) town hall
Raumtemperatur (f) room temperature
rechts right
Redakteur(in) (m/f) editor
reden to talk, to chat
Regel (f) rule
regelmäßig regular(ly)
Regen (m) rain
regnen to rain
Reihenhaus (n) terraced house
rein pure
reisen to travel
Reißverschluss (m) zip
renoviert (from **renovieren**) renovated
renovierungsbedürftig in need of renovation
reservieren to reserve
Rest (m) rest

Restaurantführer (m) restaurant guide
Resultat (n) result
Rezept (n) recipe
Rhein (m) (the river) Rhine
richtig correct
Richtung (f) direction
Risiko (n) risk
Rock (m) skirt
Römer (pl) Romans
rot red
Rotkohl (m) red cabbage
Rücken (m) back
Rucksack (m) rucksack
Ruf (m) reputation
ruft ... an (from **anrufen**) calls (on the telephone)
ruhen to rest
ruhig quiet
Rum (m) rum
runter down

S

Saal (m) hall
sag mal (informal) tell me
sagen to say
Sahne (f) cream
Salz (n) salt
salzig salty
sanft gentle
Sänger(in) (m/f) singer
Schauer (m) shower
scheußlich dreadful
Schiff (n): **mit dem Schiff** by ship
schlafen to sleep
Schlafplatz (m) sleeping place
Schlafzimmer (n) bedroom
schlage ... vor (from **vorschlagen**) (I) suggest
schlank slim
schlecht bad
schließen to close
Schloss (n) castle
schmecken to taste, to like (the taste)
schmelzen to melt
Schmerzen haben to be in pain
Schmerzmittel (n) pain killer
Schnäuzer (m) moustache
schneiden to cut
schneien to snow
schnell fast

Schnitzel (n) escalope
schon einmal ever before
schon lange in a long time
schrecklich awful(ly)
schreiben to write
Schuh (m) shoe
Schulter (f) shoulder
Schwager (m) brother-in-law
Schwangerschaft (f) pregnancy
schwarz black
Schweinebraten (m) roast pork
Schweiz (f) Switzerland
Schwester (f) sister
Schwiegermutter (f) mother-in-law
Schwiegersohn (m) son-in-law
Schwiegertochter (f) daughter-in-law
Schwiegervater (m) father-in-law
schwierig difficult
Schwimmbad (n) swimming pool
schwimmen to swim
See (m) lake
segeln to sail
sehe ... fern (from fernsehen) (I) watch TV
sehen to see
sehenswert worth seeing
sehr very
seid (from sein) (you, informal, pl) are
Seide (f) silk
sein to be
sein, seine his, its
seit (dat.) since, for
Seite (f) side
    auf der linken/rechten Seite on the left/right
Seitenfach (n) side compartment/pocket
Sekretär(in) (m/f) secretary
Sekt (m) sparkling wine
separat separate(ly)
servieren to serve
Sesambrötchen (n) sesame seed roll
sicher sure(ly), certain(ly)
sie (sing) she, it
sie (pl) they

Sie you (sing/pl, formal)
sieht ... aus (from aussehen) (he/she/it) looks (like)
sind (from sein) are
singen to sing
SMS (f) text message
so so
so gegen around (time)
sofort immediately
Sohn (m) son
sollen shall
sollten (from sollen) (we/you formal) should
Sommer (m) summer
    diesen Sommer this summer
Sommermonat (m) summer month
sondern but (rather)
Sonnabend (m) Saturday
Sonnenbrille (f) sun glasses
sonnengelb sun yellow
sonnig sunny
sonst otherwise
sozial social(ly)
Spanferkel (n) suckling pig
Spaß (m) haben to have fun
spät late
    bis später see you later
Spaziergang (m) walk
spielen to play
Spielplatz (m) playground
spirituell spiritual(ly)
sportlich casual(ly)
Sportzentrum (n) sports centre
Sprache (f) language
Sprachkurs (m) language course
Sprachreise (f) language study trip
Sprachschule (f) language school
sprechen to speak
Spülmaschine (f) dishwasher
Staat (m) state
Stadt (f) town
Stadtführer (m) city guide
Stadtkern (m) town centre
Stadtplan (m) town map
Stadtzentrum (n) town centre

stattdessen instead
stattfinden to take place
stecken to put
stehe ... auf (from aufstehen) (I) get up
stehen: jemandem stehen to suit someone
steigen to climb
stellen to place, to stand
Stellplatz (m) parking space
sterben to die
Stiefel (m) boot
Stille (f) peace and quiet
stimme ... zu (from zustimmen) (I) agree
stimmen: das stimmt that's correct
Stoff (m) material
stornieren to cancel
Strand (m) beach
Straße (f) street, road
Stück (n) piece
Stückchen (n) small piece
studieren to study
Stunde (f) hour
suchen to look for, to seek
Süden (m) South
Südosten (m) Southeast
südwestlich Southwest
surfen to surf
süß sweet
sympathisch nice

T

Tablette (f) tablet
Tag (m) day
    jeden Tag every day
Tagesdosis (f) daily dose
täglich daily
Tal (n) valley
Tante (f) aunt
tanzen to dance
Tanzstunde (f) dance lesson
Tasche (f) bag
Taschenlampe (f) torch
Tasse (f) cup
tauschen to exchange
Teig (m) dough
Teil (m) part
teilnehmen an to take part in, to participate in
Telefonnummer (f) telephone number
Temperatur (f) temperature

Termin (m) appointment, meeting
Terrasse (f) patio, terrace
teuer expensive
Theater (n) theatre
Thema (n) topic
therapeutisch therapeutic
Thermalquellen (pl) thermal springs
Therme (pl) hot springs
Tisch (m) table
Tischler(in) (m/f) carpenter
Tischtennis (m) table tennis
Tochter (f) daughter
Toilette (f) toilet
toll great, amazing
Tor (n) gate
total total(ly)
Tourismus (m) tourism
Tourist(in) (m/f) tourist
Touristeninformation (f) tourist information
traditionell traditional
tragen to wear
tragisch tragic
Trainer(in) (m/f) coach, trainer
trainieren to work out, train
Transportmittel (pl): **öffentliche Transportmittel** public transport
treffen to meet
  sich treffen to meet up with someone
trinken to drink
trocken dry
Tropfen (m) drop
Tschechische Republik (f) Czech Republic
tschüs bye
tun to do
Türkei (f) Turkey
Typ (m) bloke

U

über (acc./dat.) over, above, across
überhaupt nicht not at all
sich überlegen (dat.) to reflect, to think about
überqueren to cross
überschreiten to exceed
übertreiben to exaggerate
Uhr (f) o'clock, clock, watch
  um wieviel Uhr? (at) what time?
Uhrzeit (f) time
um (acc.) at (time)
umfassen to include
Umfrage (f) survey
sich umsehen to browse
umtauschen to exchange
Umwelttechnik (f) clean technology
und and
Unfall (m) accident
unfreundlich unfriendly
ungefähr approximately
unhöflich rude
Universität (f) university
unpraktisch impractical
uns us, to us
unser(e) (f/m) our
unter (acc./dat.) under, among
untere(r/s) (f/m/n) lower
Unterkunft (f) accommodation
Unterwassermassage (f) hydrotherapy
Unterzeichnende(r) (f/m) signatory
Urgroßvater (m) great grandfather
Urlaub (m) holiday
  auf Urlaub on holiday
Ursache (f) reason, cause
  keine Ursache don't mention it, you're welcome

V

Valentinstag (m) Valentine's Day
Vanillesoße (f) custard
Veranstaltung (f) event
verbringen to spend (time)
Vereinigte Staaten (pl) United States
Verfügung (f) disposal
  zur Verfügung stehen to be available
vergessen to forget
Vergnügen (n) pleasure
Verhandlungsbasis (f) asking price
verheiratet married
Verkauf (m) sale

verkaufen to sell
verlassen to leave
verlässt (from **verlassen**) (he/she/it) leaves
verlieren to lose
Verlobte(r) (f/m) fiancée/fiancé
Verlust (m) loss
Verlustanzeige (f) loss report
vermieten to let, rent out
vermischen to mix
verpassen to miss (out on something)
verrühren to mix, to stir together
verschieden different, various
sich verspäten to be delayed
Verständnis (n) understanding
verstärkt reinforced
verstaucht sprained
verstehen to understand
viel a lot, much
viele many
Vielfalt (f) variety
vielleicht perhaps
Viertel (n) quarter
Vogelschutzgebiet (n) bird sanctuary
voll full
vollmundig full-bodied
von (dat.) from, of, by
vor (acc./dat.) before, to, in front of
voraus: im voraus in advance
vordere(r/s) (f/m/n) front
Vorname (m) first name
vorschlagen to suggest
Vorspeise (f) starter
vorstellen to introduce
  sich ... vorstellen (dat.) to imagine ...
Vortrag (m) speech
Vorwahl (f) dialling code

W

wache ... auf (from **aufwachen**) (I) wake up
wählen to choose, to select
während while

wandern to hike, ramble
wandern gehen to go rambling
Wanderschuhe (m pl) walking boots
Wanderung (f) hike, walk
Wanderurlaub (m) walking holiday
wann when
war (from **sein**) (I, he/she/ it) was
waren (from **sein**) (we, they, you, formal) were
warm warm
warst (from **sein**) (you, informal, sing) were
warum why
was what, which
Was für ein(e) ...! What a ...!
waschbar washable
Waschmaschine (f) washing machine
Wasser (n) water
Wasserbehandlung (f) hydrotherapy
wasserfest waterproof
Wassersport (m) water sport
Wassersportarten (pl) types of water sport
Webdesigner(in) (m/f) web designer
wechselhaft changeable
weder ... noch neither ... nor
Weg (m) path, way
weg away
wegen because of
wehtun to hurt
Weihnachten (n) Christmas
weil because
Wein (m) wine
Weingut (n) vineyard
Weinprobe (f) wine tasting
weiß white
weit far
welche(r/s) (f/m/n) which
Wellnessurlaub (m) spa holiday
Wellness-Zentrum (n) wellness centre
Welt (f) world
aus der ganzen Welt from all over the world

weltbekannt world famous
Weltkrieg (m) world war
Weltkulturerbe (n) world heritage
wem (to/with) whom
wenn if, whenever
werden to become
Weste (f) waistcoat
Westen (m) West
Wetter (n) weather
Wetterbericht (m) weather report
Wettervorhersage (f) weather forecast
wichtig important
wie how, what, as
Wie geht es Ihnen? How are you? (formal)
Wie geht's? how are you? (informal)
Wie ist ...? What is ... like?
Wie schade! What a pity!
Wie schön! How lovely, nice!
wie viele how many
wieder again
wiederholen to repeat
Wiederhören (n): **auf Wiederhören** goodbye (on the telephone)
wiederkommen to come back
Wiedersehen (n): **auf Wiedersehen** good-bye
windig windy
windsurfen to go windsurfing
Wintersporturlaub (m) winter sports holiday
Wintersportwetter (n) winter sports weather
Winzer (m) winegrower
Winzerfest (n) wine festival
wir we
wirklich really, truly
wirksam effective(ly)
wissen to know things or facts
wissen lassen to let (someone) know
Witwe(r) (f/m) widow(er)
wo where
Woche (f) week
Wochenende (n) weekend

Wochenrate (f) weekly rate
woher where ... from
wohin where ... (to)
Wohlbefinden (n) well-being
wohnen to live
wohnhaft in resident in
Wohnküche (f) kitchen-living room
Wohnort (m) domicile, residence
Wohnung (f) flat, apartment
Wohnzimmer (n) living room, lounge
Wolle (f) wool
wunderbar wonderful
wunderschön beautiful
wünschen to wish
Wurst (f) sausage

Z

zahlen to pay
Zeichen (n) sign, tone, signal
zeichnen to draw
zeigen to show
Zeitspanne (f) period
zentral central(ly)
Zentrale (f) head office
Zentralheizung (f) central heating
ziehen to move, to relocate
ziemlich quite, rather
Zimmer (n) room
zu (dat.) to, too
Zubehör (n) accessories
zubereiten to prepare, to cook
zuerst first of all
Zug (m) train
mit dem Zug by train
zuhause at home
von zuhause from home
Zum Wohl! To your health!
zurückkehren to return
zusammen together
zustimmen to agree
Zweifamilienhaus (n) two-family house
zweimal twice
Zwiebel (f) onion
zwischen (acc./dat.) between

English–German glossary

A

above **über** (acc./dat.)
accident **Unfall** (m)
to accommodate **beherbergen**
accommodation **Unterkunft** (f)
accountant **Buchhalter(in)** (m/f)
across **über** (acc./dat.)
activity holiday **Aktivurlaub** (m)
acupuncture **Akkupunktur** (f)
adult **Erwachsene(r)** (f/m)
advance: in advance **im voraus**
after **nach** (dat.)
afternoon **Nachmittag** (m) in the afternoons **nachmittags**
again **wieder**
ago **vor**
to agree **zustimmen**
air conditioning **Klimaanlage** (f)
airline **Fluggesellschaft** (f)
alcohol **Alkohol** (m)
all **alle**
allergic to **allergisch gegen**
allowed: to be allowed to (may) **dürfen**
alone **alleine**
Alps **Alpen** (pl)
also **auch**
although **obwohl**
always **immer**
amazing **toll**
America **Amerika** (n)
American national **Amerikaner(in)** (m/f)
and **und**
ankle **Knöchel** (m)
anniversary **Jubiläum** (n)
another **ein anderer/eine andere** (m/f)
answer **Antwort** (f)
any more **mehr**
apartment **Wohnung** (f)
aperitif **Aperitif** (m)
apple **Apfel** (m)
appointment **Termin** (m)
approximately **etwa, ungefähr**

are **bist/sind/seid**
area **Gebiet** (n)
arm **Arm** (m)
around (time) **so gegen**
to arrive **ankommen** (pp **angekommen**)
art **Kunst** (f)
arthritis **Arthritis** (f)
as **als, wie**
as far as **bis** (acc.)
asthma **Asthma** (n)
at **an** (acc./dat.), **bei** (dat.), (time) **um** (acc.)
aunt **Tante** (f)
Australia **Australien** (n)
Austria **Österreich** (n)
autumn **Herbst** (m)
available **frei**
 to be available **zur Verfügung stehen**
avenue **Allee** (f)
average **Durchschnitt** (m)
away **entfernt, weg**
awful(ly) **schrecklich**

B

back **Rücken** (m)
bad **schlecht**
badminton **Federball** (m)
bag **Tasche** (f)
bakery **Bäckerei** (f)
banana **Banane** (f)
bank **Bank** (f)
banker **Bankier(in)** (m/f)
barbecue **Grillparty** (f)
basement **Keller** (m)
bath **Bad** (n)
bathroom **Badezimmer** (n)
to be **sein**
beach **Strand** (m)
beautiful **schön, wunderschön**
because **denn, weil**
bed **Bett** (n)
 to go to bed **ins Bett gehen**
bedroom **Schlafzimmer** (n)
beer **Bier** (n)
before **vor** (acc./dat.)
to begin **beginnen**
behind **hinter** (acc./dat.)
to believe **glauben**
beside **neben** (acc./dat.)
best (of all) **am besten, am liebsten**

best wishes **mit freundlichen Grüßen**
better **besser**
between **zwischen** (acc/dat)
bicycle tour **Fahrradtour** (f)
big **groß**
bike: by bike **mit dem Fahrrad** (n)
binoculars **Fernglas** (n)
birthday **Geburtstag** (m)
bit: a bit **ein bisschen**
black **schwarz**
blonde **blond**
blue **blau**
to boil **kochen**
book **Buch** (n)
to book **buchen, reservieren**
booking **Reservierung** (f)
boot **Stiefel** (m)
born **geboren**
bought **gekauft**
bowling/to go bowling **kegeln**
bowling alley **Kegelbahn** (f)
boyfriend **Freund**
Brazil **Brasilien** (n)
bread **Brot** (n)
bread roll **Brötchen** (n)
break **Pause** (f)
to break (bone) **brechen** (pp **gebrochen**)
breathtaking(ly) **atemberaubend**
bright **bunt**
to bring **bringen** (pp **gebracht**)
brochure **Broschüre** (f)
broken **defekt, gebrochen**
brother **Bruder** (m)
brother-in-law **Schwager** (m)
brown **braun**
browsing: I am just browsing **ich sehe mich nur um**
bruised **geprellt**
builder **Baumeister(in)** (m/f)
bus **Bus** (m)
bus stop **Bushaltestelle** (f)
but **aber, (rather) sondern**
butter **Butter** (f)
to buy **kaufen**
by **bei** (dat.), **von** (dat.)
bye **tschüs**

C

cake **Kuchen** (m)
calendar **Kalender** (m)
to call (on the telephone)
anrufen (pp **angerufen**)
called: to be called **heißen**
camera **Kamera** (f)
camping **Camping** (n)
campsite **Campingplatz** (m)
can (to be able to) **können**
to cancel **stornieren**
capsule **Kapsel** (f)
car: by car **mit dem Auto** (n)
car space **Stellplatz** (m)
Caribbean **Karibik** (f)
carnival **Karneval** (m)
carpenter **Tischler(in)** (m/f)
cash **Geld** (n)
cash machine
Geldautomat (m)
castle **Schloss** (n)
casual(ly) (clothes) **sportlich**
casualty department
Notaufnahme (f)
cathedral **Dom** (m)
celebration **Fest** (n), **Feier** (f)
cellar **Keller** (m)
central heating
Zentralheizung (f)
central(ly) **zentral**
centre **Kern** (m)
cheap **billig**
Cheers! **Prosit!, Prost!**
chemist (person)
Apotheker(in) (m/f)
chemist's **Apotheke** (f)
child **Kind** (n)
Christmas **Weihnachten** (n)
chubby **mollig**
cider **Apfelwein** (m)
cinema **Kino** (n)
city (big) **Großstadt** (f)
city guide **Stadtführer**
class **Klasse** (f)
to climb **steigen** (pp
gestiegen)
to close **schließen**
cloudy **bewölkt**
coast **Küste** (f)
coffee **Kaffee** (m)
cold **kalt**
cold syrup
Erkältungssirup (m)
colour **Farbe** (f)
to come **kommen**
(pp **gekommen**)

comfortable **bequem,
komfortabel**, (cosy)
gemütlich
to commute **pendeln**
company **Firma** (f)
complete(ly) **komplett**
compliment(s)
Kompliment (n)
concert **Konzert** (n)
conference **Konferenz** (f)
Congratulations!
Herzlichen Glückwunsch!
contact **Kontakt** (m)
to contain **enthalten**
cook **Koch/Köchin** (m/f)
to cook **kochen,
zubereiten**
corner **Ecke** (f)
correct **richtig**
   that's correct **das stimmt**
to cost **kosten**
cotton **Baumwolle** (f)
cough **Husten** (m)
cough syrup
Hustensaft (m)
country: to the country
aufs Land
country(side) **Land** (n)
course (meal) **Gang** (m),
(study programme) **Kurs** (m)
cousin **Cousin** (m), **Cusine** (f)
cream **Sahne** (f)
credit card **Kreditkarte** (f)
to cross **überqueren**
cuisine **Küche** (f)
culture **Kultur** (f)
cup **Tasse** (f)
curiosity: out of curiosity
aus Neugier (f)
curly **lockig**
to cut **schneiden**
cycle path **Radweg** (m)

D

daily **täglich**
to dance **tanzen**
dance lesson **Tanzstunde** (f)
dark **dunkel**
dark blue **dunkelblau**
dark-haired **dunkelhaarig**
date **Datum** (n)
date of birth
Geburtsdatum (n)
daughter **Tochter** (f)
daughter-in-law
Schwiegertochter (f)

day **Tag** (m)
dear **liebe(r)** (f/m)
(informal), **sehr geehrte(r)**
(f/m) (formal)
to decide **sich entscheiden**
(pp **entschieden**)
degree **Grad** (m)
delicate **delikat**
Denmark **Dänemark** (n)
deposit **Kaution** (f)
to describe **beschreiben**
design **Design** (n)
dessert **Nachspeise** (f)
detached house
Einfamilienhaus (n)
dialling code **Vorwahl** (f)
diet **Diät** (f)
different **verschiedene**
difficult **schwierig**
dining room **Esszimmer** (n)
dinner **Abendessen** (n)
direction **Richtung** (f)
disco **Disko** (f)
discount **Ermäßigung** (f)
dishwasher
Spülmaschine (f)
divorced **geschieden**
to do **tun, machen**
doctor **Arzt/Ärztin** (m/f),
Doktor(in) (m/f)
don't mention it **keine
Ursache**
dose **Dosis** (f)
down **runter**
dreadful **furchtbar,
scheußlich**
dress **Kleid** (n)
to dress (oneself) **sich
kleiden**
to drink **trinken**
(pp **getrunken**)
driving licence
Führerschein (m)
drop **Tropfen** (m)
dry **trocken**
dumpling **Kloß, Knödel** (m)

E

ear **Ohr** (n)
earache
Ohrenschmerzen (pl)
earlier **früher**
early **früh**
east **Osten** (m)
to eat **essen** (pp **gegessen**)
editor **Redakteur(in)** (m/f)

egg **Ei** (n)
elegant **elegant**
emergency doctor
Notarzt (m)
end **Ende** (n)
to end **beenden**
England **England**
English **englisch**, (language)
Englisch
Englishman/woman
Engländer(in) (m/f)
to enjoy **genießen**
  enjoy your meal **guten**
Appetit
  enjoy your stay **guten**
Aufenthalt
to enjoy oneself **sich**
amüsieren
enough **genug**
entrance hall
Eingangshalle (f)
equipment **Ausstattung** (f)
escalope **Schnitzel** (n)
estate agent
Immobilienmakler(in) (m/f)
European **europäisch**
evening **Abend** (m)
  in the evenings **abends**
  this evening **heute**
Abend
ever before **schon einmal**
every **jede(r), alle**
  every day **jeden Tag**
  every year **jedes Jahr**
everything **alles**
excellent(ly) **ausgezeichnet**
to exchange **(um)tauschen**
excursion **Ausflug** (m)
excuse me **entschuldigen**
Sie (mich)
to exist **existieren**
expensive **teuer**
to explore **erkunden**
extreme sports
Extremsport (m)
eye **Auge** (n)
eye drops **Augentropfen** (pl)

F
to fall **fallen** (pp **gefallen**)
family **Familie** (f)
to fancy **Lust haben auf**
fantastic(ally) **fantastisch,**
fabelhaft
far **weit**
farm **Bauernhof** (m)
fashion **Mode** (f)
fashionable **modisch**

fast **schnell**
fat **dick**
father-in-law
Schwiegervater (m)
favourite **Lieblings**
to feel well: **gut gehen**
  I feel well: **es geht mir**
gut/mir geht es gut
ferry **Fähre** (f)
festival **Fest** (n)
fever **Fieber** (n)
few: a few **ein paar, einige**
fiancée/fiancé
Verlobte(r) (f/m)
to fill in **ausfüllen**
film **Film** (m)
to find **finden**
(pp **gefunden**)
finger **Finger** (m)
to finish **beenden**
first: for the first time **zum**
ersten Mal (n)
first name **Vorname** (m)
fish **Fisch** (m)
to fish **angeln**
flat **Wohnung** (f)
flight **Flug** (m)
floor **Boden** (m), (storey)
Etage (f)
flower **Blume** (f)
flu **Grippe** (f)
to fly **fliegen**
foggy **nebelig**
food **Essen** (n)
food and wine guide
Gastronomie- und
Weinführer (m)
foot **Fuß** (m)
  on foot **zu Fuß**
football **Fußball** (m)
football match
Fußballspiel (n)
for **für** (acc.), (since) **seit**
(dat.), (because) **denn**
to forget **vergessen**
France **Frankreich** (n)
free **frei**, (of charge) **gratis,**
kostenlos
freezer **Gefrierschrank** (m)
friend **Freund(in)** (m/f)
friendly **freundlich**
from **von** (dat.), **aus** (dat.)
front **vordere(r/s)** (f/m/n)
  in front of **vor** (acc./dat.)
fruity **fruchtig**
to fry **braten**
frying pan **Pfanne** (f)
full **voll**

fun: to have fun **Spaß** (m)
haben
furnishings **Ausstattung** (f)

G

garage **Garage** (f)
garden **Garten** (m)
German **deutsch,**
(language) **Deutsch** (n),
(person) **Deutsche(r)** (f/m)
Germany **Deutschland**
to get dressed **sich**
anziehen
to get off (bus etc.)
aussteigen
to get up **aufstehen**
girlfriend **Freundin**
to give **geben**
glass **Glas** (n)
glasses (spectacles) **Brille** (f)
global **global**
to go (by vehicle) **fahren**
(pp **gefahren**), (on foot)
gehen (pp **gegangen**),
laufen (pp **gelaufen**)
  to go out **ausgehen**
(pp **ausgegangen**)
good **gut**, (favourable)
günstig
goodbye **auf Wiedersehen**
goodbye (on telephone)
auf Wiederhören
good-looking **gut**
aussehend
grandfather **Großvater** (m)
grandmother **Großmutter** (f)
grandparents **Großeltern** (pl)
grandson **Enkel** (m)
graphic designer
Grafiker(in) (m/f)
great **prima, toll**
Great Britain
Großbritannien (n)
great grandfather
Urgroßvater (m)
Greece **Griechenland** (n)
green **grün**
greetings **Grüße** (pl)
grey **grau**
grocery store
Lebensmittelgeschäft (n)
ground floor **Erdgeschoss** (n)
group **Gruppe** (f)
guided tour **Führung** (f)
gym **Fitnessstudio** (n)

H

had **hatte(st/n/t)**
hairdresser **Friseur(in)** (m/f)
half **halb**
hall **Halle** (f), **Saal** (m)
hall(way) **Diele** (f)
hamburger **Hamburger** (m)
hand **Hand** (f)
handball **Handball** (m)
to happen **passieren**
happy **froh, glücklich**
  Happy Birthday!
**Herzlichen Glückwunsch
zum Geburtstag!**
harbour **Hafen** (m)
hat **Hut** (m)
have **habe/hast/hat/haben**
to have **haben**
to have to (must) **müssen**
he **er**
head **Kopf** (m)
head chef **Chefkoch** (m)
head office **Zentrale** (f)
headache
Kopfschmerzen (pl)
headache tablets
Kopfschmerztabletten (pl)
health resort **Kurort** (m)
health spa **Heilbad** (n)
healthy/healthily **gesund**
to hear, to listen **hören**
to heat **erwärmen**
helmet **Helm** (m)
to help **helfen**
here **hier**
  (to) here **hierher**
high **hoch**
to hike **wandern**
hike **Wanderung** (f)
to hire **mieten**
hobby **Hobby** (n)
holiday **Urlaub** (m)
  on holiday **auf Urlaub**
holiday flat
Ferienwohnung (f)
holiday home
Ferienhaus (n)
home (town, land)
Heimat (f)
home: at home **zuhause**
  from home **von zuhause**
  to my/your etc. house
nach Hause
homeopathic
homöopathisch
to hope **hoffen**
horseback: on horseback
zu Pferd (n)

hospital **Krankenhaus** (n)
host family **Gastfamilie** (f)
hot **heiß**
hot springs **Therme** (pl)
hotel **Hotel** (n)
hotel guide **Hotelführer** (m)
hour **Stunde** (f)
house **Haus** (n)
how **wie**
How are you? **Wie geht's?**
(informal), **Wie geht es
Ihnen?** (formal)
how many **wie viele**
hungry: to be hungry
Hunger haben
to hurt **wehtun**
husband **Mann** (m)

I

ice cream **Eis** (n)
idea **Idee** (f)
ideal **ideal**
identity card **Ausweis** (m)
if **wenn**, (whether) **ob**
ill **krank**
immediately **sofort**
impolite **unhöflich**
important **wichtig**
impractical **unpraktisch**
in **in** (acc./dat.)
to include **umfassen**
inclusive **inklusive**
information **Information** (f)
information leaflet
Informationsblatt (n)
inhabitant
Einwohner(in) (m/f)
inn **Gaststätte** (f)
instead **stattdessen**
insurance **Versicherung** (f)
to intend to **beabsichtigen
... zu**
interested: to be interested
in **sich interessieren für**
interesting **interessant**
internet connection
Internetanschluss (m)
to introduce **vorstellen**
invitation **Einladung** (f)
to invite **einladen**
(pp **eingeladen**)
is **ist**
island **Insel** (f)
isolated **abgelegen**

J

jacket **Jacke** (f)
jeans **Jeans** (f)

journalist
Journalist(in) (m/f)
jumper **Pullover** (m)

K

kilometre **Kilometer** (m)
kind **freundlich**, (sweet)
lieb, (type) **Art** (f)
king **König** (m)
kitchen **Küche** (f)
knee **Knie** (n)
to know (people and
places) **kennen**, (things and
facts) **wissen**
  to let (someone) know
wissen lassen
kung fu: to do kung fu
Kung Fu machen

L

lake **See** (m)
language **Sprache** (f)
language course
Sprachkurs (m)
language school
Sprachschule (f)
laptop **Laptop** (m)
to last **dauern**
late **spät**
later: see you later **bis
später**
to learn **lernen**, (to acquire)
erlernen
leather **Leder** (n)
to leave **verlassen**; (a
message) **hinterlassen**,
(leave something behind)
lassen (pp **gelassen**)
left **links**
  on the left **auf der linken
Seite**
leg **Bein** (n)
leisure **Freizeit** (f)
to let **lassen**, (to rent out)
vermieten
let's **lasst uns** (inf), **lassen
Sie uns** (formal)
letter **Brief** (m)
lift **Aufzug** (m)
light **hell, leicht**
light blue **hellblau**
light brown **hellbraun**
lightweight **leicht**
like: What is ... like?
Wie ist ...?
to like **mögen**
  would like **möchte**
to like ... ing ... **gern(e)**

like: I like **mir gefällt**
like ... best **am liebsten**
linen **Leinen** (n)
list **Liste** (f)
to live **wohnen, leben**
living room
Wohnzimmer (n)
local **lokal**
location **Lage** (f), **Ort** (m)
long **lang**
   for a long time
schon lange
long-sleeved **langärmelig**
to look for **suchen**
to look like **aussehen**
to lose **verlieren**
(pp **verloren**)
loss **Verlust** (m)
loss report
Verlustanzeige (f)
lost property office
Fundbüro (n)
lot: a lot **eine Menge, viel**
to love **lieben**
   love (from) (informal)
liebe Grüße
lovely: How lovely!
Wie schön!
lunch **Mittagessen** (n)
   to have lunch **zu Mittag
essen**

M

made from **aus** (dat.)
main course **Hauptspeise** (f)
to make **machen**
man **Mann** (m)
many **viele**
map **Karte** (f)
married **verheiratet**
   to get married/marry
heiraten
martial arts **Kampfsport** (m)
marvellous **herrlich**
material **Stoff** (m)
matter: What's the matter?
Was ist los?
may (to be allowed to)
dürfen
me **mich**
   to me **mir**
meal **Mahlzeit** (f), **Essen** (n)
mean (unkind) **gemein**
medicine **Medizin** (f)
to meet **treffen**
   to meet up with someone
sich treffen
meeting **Termin** (m)

message **Nachricht** (f)
metre **Meter** (m/n)
middle: in the middle of
mitten
midnight **Mitternacht** (f)
milk **Milch** (f)
million **Million** (f)
minute **Minute** (f)
mixer **Mixer** (m)
mobile phone **Handy** (n)
moment **Augenblick** (m)
money **Geld** (m)
month **Monat** (m)
more **mehr**
morning: in the mornings
morgens
most: the most **die meisten**
mother **Mutter** (f)
mother-in-law
Schwiegermutter (f)
mountain **Berg** (m)
mountain bike
Mountainbike (n)
moustache **Schnäuzer** (m)
mouth **Mund** (m)
to move, to relocate **ziehen**
Mr **Herr** (m)
Mrs **Frau** (f)
much **viel**
museum **Museum** (n)
music **Musik** (f)
musician **Musiker(in)** (m/f)
must (to be able to)
müssen

N

name **Name** (m)
national park
Nationalpark (m)
nationality **Nationalität** (f)
nature **Natur** (f)
nature reserve
Naturschutzgebiet (n)
nature trail
Naturlehrwanderung (f)
near **neben**
nearby **in der Nähe von**
to need **brauchen**
neither ... nor **weder ...
noch**
never before **noch nie**
new **neu**
new-build **Neubau** (m)
new potatoes
Frühkartoffeln (pl)
next **nächste(r)** (f/m)
next to **neben** (acc./dat.)
nice **nett**, (person)

sympathisch
   How nice! **Wie schön!**
night: at night **nachts**
no (none) **kein** (m, n),
keine (f, pl)
no one **niemand**
normally **normalerweise**
north **Norden** (m)
nose **Nase** (f)
nose spray **Nasenspray**
(m/n)
not **nicht**
not as (adj) as **nicht so**
(adj) **wie**
not at all **gar/überhaupt
nicht**
not only ... but also **nicht
nur ... sondern auch**
not so ... **nicht so ...**
not until **erst**
not yet **noch nicht**
nothing **nichts**
now **jetzt**
number **Anzahl** (f),
Nummer (f)
nut **Nuß** (f) (pl **Nüsse**)

O

o'clock **Uhr** (f)
of **von** (dat.)
of course **natürlich**
offer **Angebot** (n)
often **oft**
okay **in Ordnung**
old **alt**
old town **Altstadt** (f)
old-fashioned **altmodisch**
omelette **Omelett** (n)
on an (acc./dat.), (date/day)
am (= an dem) (dat.), (on
top of) **auf** (dat.)
once **einmal**
onion **Zwiebel** (f)
only **nur**
onto **auf** (acc.)
to open **öffnen**
opening times
Öffnungszeiten (pl)
opera **Opernmusik** (f)
opposite **gegenüber**
or **oder**
orange **Orange** (f)
to organise **organisieren**
other **andere(r)**
out of **aus** (dat.)
outdoors **im Freien**
outside **draußen**
oven **Ofen** (m)

over **über** (acc./dat.)
owner **Besitzer(in)** (m/f)

P

pain: to be in pain
Schmerzen haben
painkiller
Schmerzmittel (n)
to paint **malen**
pale **blass**
panoramic view
Panoramablick (m)
parents **Eltern** (pl)
park **Park** (m)
part (area, piece) **Teil** (m)
partner **Partner(in)** (m/f)
party **Feier** (f)
passport **Pass** (m)
past (prep) **nach** (dat.)
path **Weg** (m)
patio **Terrasse** (f)
to pay (for something)
(be)zahlen (pp **(be)zahlt)**
peace and quiet **Stille** (f)
peak (summit) **Gipfel** (m)
pepper **Pfeffer** (m)
per **pro**
per cent **Prozent** (n)
perfect **perfekt**
perhaps **vielleicht**
period (of time)
Zeitspanne (f)
person **Mensch** (m)
personal(ly) **persönlich**
photograph **Foto** (n)
photographer
Fotograf(in) (m/f)
photography **Fotografie** (f)
piece **Stück** (n)
pile **Menge** (f)
pity: What a pity! **Wie
schade!**
place **Ort** (m)
to plan **planen**
to play **spielen**
playground **Spielplatz** (m)
please **bitte (schön)**
pleased to meet you
freut mich
pleasure **Vergnügen** (n)
  with pleasure **gern(e)**
plumber **Klempner(in)** (m/f)
pocket **Tasche** (f)
Poland **Polen** (n)
police **Polizei** (f)
police officer
Polizist(in) (m/f)

police station
Polizeirevier (n)
Polish national
Pole/Polin (m/f)
polite **höflich**
poor thing **Sie/Du Arme(r)**
(formal/informal, f/m)
Portuguese (language)
Portugiesisch (n),
(person) **Portugiese/
Portugiesin** (m/f)
possible **möglich**
postman/postwoman
Postbote/Postbotin (m/f)
potato **Kartoffel** (f)
to pour **gießen**
powder **Pulver** (n)
practical **praktisch**
prefer: I prefer... **Ich ...
lieber ...**
pregnancy
Schwangerschaft (f)
to prepare **zubereiten**
present **Geschenk** (n)
press officer
Pressesprecher(in) (m/f)
price **Preis** (m)
problem **Problem** (n)
profession: by profession
von Beruf (m)
property **Immobilie** (f)
pub **Kneipe** (f)
public **öffentlich**
pure **rein**
purse **Portemonnaie** (n)
to put **stecken**

Q

quality **Qualität** (f)
quarter **Viertel** (n)
question **Frage** (f)
quiet **ruhig**
quite **ziemlich**
quiz **Quiz** (n)

R

rain **Regen** (m)
to rain **regnen**
to ramble **wandern**
to read **lesen**
really **wirklich**
reason **Ursache** (f)
to receive **bekommen,
erhalten** (pp **erhalten**)
recipe **Rezept** (n)
to recommend **empfehlen**
red **rot**

refrigerator **Kühlschrank** (m)
region **Region** (f), **Gebiet** (n)
regular(ly) **regelmäßig**
(the river) Rhine **Rhein** (m)
to relax **sich entspannen**
to remember
sich merken (dat.)
to remind **erinnern an**
remote **abgelegen**
renovated **renoviert**
to rent **mieten**
to repeat **wiederholen**
reply **Antwort** (f)
report **Anzeige** (f)
to report (an incident) **eine
Anzeige machen**
request **Anfrage** (f)
to reserve **reservieren,
buchen**
rest **Rest** (m)
to rest **ruhen**
restaurant **Restaurant** (n),
Gaststätte (f)
restaurant guide
Restaurantführer (m)
result **Resultat** (n)
to return **zurückkehren**
right **rechts**
  on the right **auf der
rechten Seite**
road **Straße** (f)
roast **geröstet**
roast pork
Schweinebraten (m)
room **Zimmer** (n)
rosé **rosé**
rucksack **Rucksack** (m)
rude **unhöflich**
rule **Regel** (f)
rum **Rum** (m)
to run **laufen** (pp **gelaufen**)

S

to sail **segeln**
sale **Verkauf** (m)
salt **Salz** (n)
salty **salzig**
Saturday **Samstag** (m),
Sonnabend (m)
sausage **Wurst** (f)
to say **sagen**
to say **du** to each other
sich duzen
scared: to be scared
Angst haben
sea(side) **Meer** (n)
secretary **Sekretär(in)** (m/f)

to see **sehen** (pp **gesehen**)
to sell **verkaufen**
semi-dry **halbtrocken**
seminar **Seminar** (n)
separate(ly) **separat**
serious **ernst**
shall **sollen**
to shave (oneself) **sich rasieren**
ship: by ship **mit dem Schiff** (n)
shirt **Hemd** (n)
shoe **Schuh** (m)
shop **Geschäft** (n)
shopping: to go shopping **einkaufen gehen**
shopping centre **Einkaufszentrum** (n)
short **kurz**
short break **Kurzurlaub** (m)
should **sollte(st/n/t)**
shoulder **Schulter** (f)
to show **zeigen**
shower **Dusche** (f), (weather) **Schauer** (m)
shower: to have a shower **sich duschen**
side **Seite** (f)
side pocket **Seitentasche** (f)
silk **Seide** (f)
since **seit** (dat.)
to sing **singen**
singer **Sänger(in)** (m/f)
single bed **Einzelbett** (n)
sister **Schwester** (f)
situation **Situation** (f)
size **Größe** (f)
skirt **Rock** (m)
to sleep **schlafen** (pp **geschlafen**)
sleeve **Ärmel** (m)
slim **schlank**
slow(ly) **langsam**
small **klein**
to smile **lächeln**
to snow **schneien**
so **so**
social(ly) **sozial**
some **einige**
someone **jemand**
something **etwas**
sometimes **manchmal**
son **Sohn** (m)
son-in-law **Schwiegersohn** (m)
soon **bald**
sore throat **Halsschmerzen** (pl)

sorry: I am sorry **(es) tut mir leid**
south **Süden** (m)
spa holiday **Wellnessurlaub** (m)
spa resort **Heil- und Kurort** (m)
spacious **geräumig**
spare time **Freizeit** (f)
sparkling wine **Sekt** (m)
to speak **sprechen**
to spend (time) **verbringen**
spoon **Löffel** (m)
sport **Sport** (m)
sports centre **Sportzentrum** (n)
sprained **verstaucht**
square (in town) **Platz** (m)
stamp **Briefmarke** (f)
to stand **stellen**
starter **Vorspeise** (f)
state **Staat** (m)
station **Bahnhof** (m)
to stay **bleiben**
still **immer noch**
stomach **Magen** (m)
stomach ache **Magenschmerzen** (pl)
straight **glatt**
straight on **geradeaus**
street **Straße** (f)
to study **studieren**
sturdy **fest**
stop (bus, tram etc.) **Haltestelle** (f)
style **Art** (f)
   of this style **in dieser Art** (f)
to suffer from **leiden an**
to suggest **vorschlagen**
to suit someone **jemandem stehen**
summer **Sommer** (m)
   this summer **diesen Sommer**
sunglasses **Sonnenbrille** (f)
sunny **sonnig**
superb(ly) **ausgezeichnet**
supermarket **Supermarkt** (m)
supper **Abendessen** (n)
   to have supper **zu Abend essen**
to surf **surfen**
surgeon **Chirurg(in)** (m/f)
surname **Nachname** (m)
sweatshirt **Sweatshirt** (n)
sweet (wine) **lieblich,**

(person, taste) **süß**
to swim **schwimmen**
swimming pool **Schwimmbad** (n)
Switzerland **Schweiz** (f)

T

table **Tisch** (m)
table tennis **Tischtennis** (m)
tablet **Tablette** (f)
to take **nehmen**, (medication) **einnehmen**
to take photos **fotografieren**
to take place **stattfinden**
to talk **reden**
tall **groß**
taste **Geschmack** (m)
to taste **schmecken, probieren**
to taste good **schmecken**
telephone number **Telefonnummer** (f)
to tell **mitteilen**
tell me **sag mal** (informal)
temperature **Temperatur** (f)
terrace **Terrasse** (f)
terraced house **Reihenhaus** (n)
text message **SMS** (f)
than **als**
to thank **danken**
thank you **danke**
that **dass, diese(r)(s)** (f/m/n)
theatre **Theater** (n)
then **dann**
there **dort**
   to be there **da sein**
   (to) there **dorthin**
there is/are **es gibt**
there was/were **es gab**
thermal springs **Thermalquellen** (pl)
these **diese**
thin **dünn**
to think **glauben**
think of **halte(n/t)/hält(st)** **... von**
this **diese(r)(s)** (f/m/n)
those **diese**
throat **Hals** (m)
throat lozenge **Halspastille** (f)
through **durch**
thunderstorm **Gewitter** (n)
tie **Krawatte** (f)
tight **eng**

time: (at) what time? **um wieviel Uhr?**
tired **müde**
to (town, country) **nach** (dat.), (time) **vor** (dat.) (building) **zu** (dat)
To your health! **Zum Wohl!**
toast **Toast** (m)
today **heute**
together **zusammen**
toilet **Toilette** (f)
tomorrow **morgen**
too (as well) **auch, zu**
top **Top** (n)
torch **Taschenlampe** (f)
tourist information **Touristeninformation** (f)
tourist office **Fremdenverkehrsamt** (n)
towel **Handtuch** (n)
town **Stadt** (f), **Stadtkern** (m)
town centre **Stadtkern** (m), **Stadtzentrum** (n)
town hall **Rathaus** (n)
town map **Stadtplan** (m)
traditional **traditionell**
traffic lights **Ampel** (f)
train **Bahn** (f), **Zug** (m)
  by train **mit dem Zug**
to train **trainieren**
to travel **reisen, fahren** (pp **gefahren**)
treatment, therapy **Behandlung** (f)
tree **Baum** (m)
trip **Ausflug** (m)
trousers **Hose** (f)
to try **probieren**
to try on **anprobieren**
T-shirt **T-Shirt** (n)
twice **zweimal**
type: of this type **in dieser Art** (f)

U

uncle **Onkel** (m)
under **unter** (acc./dat.)
to understand **verstehen** (pp **verstanden**)
unfortunately **leider**
unfriendly **unfreundlich**
United States **Vereinigte Staaten** (pl)
university **Universität** (f)
until **bis** (acc.)
  until later **bis später**
  until now **bis jetzt**

up to **bis zu** (dat.)
(to) us **uns**
useful **nützlich**
utility room **Abstellraum** (m)

V

valley **Tal** (n)
variety **Vielfalt** (f)
vegetables **Gemüse** (n)
very **sehr**
view **Aussicht** (f), **Blick** (m)
villa **Ferienhaus** (n)
village **Dorf** (n)
vineyard **Weingut** (n)
to visit **besichtigen, besuchen**

W

waiter/waitress **Kellner(in)** (m/f)
to wake up **aufwachen**
(I) wake up **wache ... auf**
to walk **laufen** (pp **gelaufen**)
walk **Spaziergang** (m)
walking boots **Wanderschuhe** (pl)
walking holiday **Wanderurlaub** (m)
wall **Mauer** (f)
wallet **Brieftasche** (f)
warm **warm**
was **war**
washing machine **Waschmaschine** (f)
to watch TV **fernsehen** (pp **ferngesehen**)
water **Wasser** (n)
water sport(s) **Wassersport** (m), **Wassersportarten** (pl)
waterproof **wasserfest**
way **Weg** (m)
we **wir**
to wear **tragen**
weather **Wetter** (n)
weather forecast **Wettervorhersage** (f)
web designer **Webdesigner(in)** (m/f)
week **Woche** (f)
weekend **Wochenende** (n)
weekly rate **Wochenrate** (f)
welcome: you're welcome **keine Ursache** (f)
well-being **Wohlbefinden** (n)
were **war(st/en/t)**

west **Westen** (m)
wet **nass**
what **was**
when **wann**, (talking about past) **als**
where **wo**
where from **woher**
where (to) **wohin**
which **welche(r/s)** (f/m/n)
while **während**
white **weiß**
why **warum**
widow(er) **Witwe(r)** (f/m)
wife **Frau** (f)
wildlife **Flora und Fauna** (f)
windsurfing: to go windsurfing **windsurfen**
windy **windig**
wine **Wein** (m)
wine festival **Winzerfest** (n)
wine tasting **Weinprobe** (f)
winter **Winter** (m)
winter sports holiday **Wintersporturlaub** (m)
with **mit** (dat.)
to withdraw money **Geld abheben**
without **ohne** (acc.)
woman **Frau** (f)
wonderful **wunderbar**
wool **Wolle** (f)
work **Arbeit** (f)
to work **arbeiten**
to work out **trainieren**
world **Welt** (f)
would like **möchte**
to write **schreiben** (pp **geschrieben**)
wrong **falsch**

Y

year **Jahr** (n)
  last year **letztes Jahr**
  next year **nächstes Jahr**
  this year **dieses/in diesem Jahr**
yellow **gelb**
yesterday **gestern**
young **jung**

Z

zip **Reißverschluss** (m)
zoo **Zoo** (m)